D0429468

COOK'S KITCHEN

Cakes
and
Desserts

igloobooks

igloobooks

Published in 2017
by Igloo Books Ltd
Cottage Farm
Sywell
NN6 0BJ
www.igloobooks.com

Food photography and recipe development: PhotoCuisine UK
Front and back cover images © PhotoCuisine UK

Cover designed by Nicholas Gage
Designed by Stephen Jorgensen
Edited by Caroline Icke

STA002 0617
2 4 6 8 10 9 7 5 3
ISBN: 978-1-78557-100-8

Printed and manufactured in China

Contents

Cakes and Gateaux

Victoria Sponge

SERVES 6–8

PREPARATION TIME 40 MINUTES

COOKING TIME 25 MINUTES

INGREDIENTS

120 g / 4 oz / ½ cup butter,
    at room temperature

120 g / 4 oz / ½ cup caster (superfine) sugar

2 eggs

1 tsp vanilla extract

120 g / 4 oz / ½ cup self-raising flour

250 ml / 1/2 pint / 1 cup double (heavy) cream

raspberry or strawberry jam (jelly)

icing (confectioners') sugar, to dust

METHOD

- Preheat the oven to 160°C (140°C fan) / 325F / gas 3. Grease and line two 18 cm (7 in) round sponge tins.

- Cream the butter and sugar together until pale and creamy.

- Whisk the eggs thoroughly, then beat into the butter mixture a little at a time until fully incorporated.

- Stir in the vanilla extract, then gradually sieve the flour into the bowl and fold in with a metal spoon. If the batter is too thick, add a little hot water to loosen.

- Spoon into the tins, then bake for 25 minutes or until springy and golden.

- Leave to cool for 10 minutes, then remove from the tins and cool on a wire rack.

- Whisk the cream into soft peaks. Sandwich the sponges together with the jam and cream and dust with icing sugar to serve.

TOP TIP

Replace the jam with chopped fresh strawberries for a seasonal treat.

Black Forest Gateau

SERVES 4

PREPARATION TIME 1 HOUR

COOKING TIME 25 MINUTES

INGREDIENTS

250 g / 9 oz / 1 cup butter, softened

250 g / 9 oz / 1 cup caster (superfine) sugar

150 g / 5 oz / ⅔ cup self-raising flour

3 tbsp cocoa powder

1 tsp baking powder

4 eggs

350 g / 12 oz / 1 ½ cups morello cherry
     jam (jelly)

1 jar or can bottled cherries and their juice

3 tbsp kirsch

500 ml / 1 pint / 2 cups double (heavy) cream

50 g / 1 ¾ oz / ¼ cup dark chocolate, grated

METHOD

- Preheat the oven to 190°C (170°C fan) / 375F / gas 5. Grease and line three 20 cm (8 in) round sandwich tins.

- Mix the butter, sugar, flour, cocoa powder, baking powder and eggs in a food processor until smooth.

- Divide equally between the baking tins and bake for 25 minutes until risen. Turn onto a wire rack and leave to cool completely.

- Heat the jam with the cherries and kirsch for 5 minutes, then leave to cool. Spread over two of the sponges.

- Whisk 300 ml / 10 fl. oz / 1 ¼ cups of the cream into soft peaks.

- Transfer one cherry-topped sponge to a plate, then smooth on half of the whipped cream. Sprinkle with chocolate.

- Top with the other cherry-topped sponge and repeat. Place the final clean sponge on top.

- Whisk the remaining cream into soft peaks. Smooth over the cake top and sides with a palette knife and decorate with the grated chocolate.

TOP TIP

Shave chocolate with a peeler to make chocolate curls to decorate.

Chocolate Fudge Cake

SERVES 8–10

PREPARATION TIME 30 MINUTES

COOKING TIME 30 MINUTES

INGREDIENTS

120 g / 4 oz / ½ cup self-raising flour

1 tsp baking powder

120 g / 4 oz / ½ cup butter, softened

120 g / 4 oz / ½ cup caster (superfine) sugar

2 eggs

1 ½ tbsp cocoa powder

FOR THE FILLING AND ICING

75 g / 2 ½ oz / ⅓ cup granulated sugar

75 ml / 2 ½ oz / ⅓ cup evaporated milk

120 g / 4 oz / ½ cup dark chocolate, chopped

40 g / 1 oz butter, softened

25 g / 1 oz chocolate, shaved

METHOD

- Preheat the oven to 170°C (150°C fan) / 325F / gas 3. Grease and line two 18 cm (7 in) cake tins.

- Sieve the flour and baking powder into a large bowl, then add the other cake ingredients and mix well.

- Divide the mixture equally between the cake tins and cook for 30 minutes.

- Remove the sponges from the tins and cool on a wire rack.

- To make the icing, combine the sugar and evaporated milk in a pan and stir to dissolve the sugar.

- Bring to the boil and simmer for 5 minutes, then stir in the chocolate and butter. Chill for at least 1 hour until it has thickened and is spreadable.

- Use the icing to sandwich the cakes together, then smooth the remainder over the top and sides with a palette knife. Decorate with chocolate shavings.

TOP TIP

Spread a thick layer of raspberry jam (jelly) in the middle of the two sponges.

Chocolate Ganache Gateau

SERVES 10–12

PREPARATION TIME 10 MINUTES

COOKING TIME 45–50 MINUTES

INGREDIENTS

110 g / 4 oz / ⅔ cup self-raising flour

28 g / 1 oz / ¼ cup unsweetened cocoa powder

1 tsp baking powder

110 g / 4 oz / ½ cup caster (superfine) sugar

110 g / 4 oz / ½ cup butter

2 large eggs

FOR THE GANACHE

300 ml / 10 ½ fl. oz / 1 ¼ cups double (heavy) cream

300 g / 10 ½ oz dark chocolate, chopped

75 g / 2 ½ oz / ⅓ cup butter, cubed

100 g / 3 ½ oz white chocolate

METHOD

- Preheat the oven to 180°C (160°C fan) / 355F / gas 4 and grease and line a 20 cm (8 in) round spring-form cake tin.

- Whisk together all of the cake ingredients until thoroughly combined.

- Scrape the mixture into the tin and bake for 30–35 minutes. The cake is ready when a toothpick inserted in the centre comes out clean.

- Transfer the cake to a wire rack to cool completely, then slice in half horizontally.

- For the ganache, bring the cream to a simmer, then pour it over the chocolate and stir until smooth. Blend in the butter with a stick blender.

- Clean the cake tin and line with cling film. Put one cake layer in the tin and pour over half of the ganache.

- Top with the second cake layer and pour the rest of the ganache on top. Level the surface and chill for 4 hours.

- Melt the white chocolate in a microwave or bain-marie and spread it onto a clean chopping board or marble slab.

- When it has set, but before it becomes brittle, use a peeler to make it into curls. When the ganache is set, remove the cake from the tin and top with chocolate curls before serving.

TOP TIP

When making the ganache substitute 100 ml / 3 fl. oz of cream for passion fruit juice.

Chocolate and Pecan Bundt Cake

SERVES 8–10

PREPARATION TIME 5 MINUTES

COOKING TIME 45 MINUTES

INGREDIENTS

225 g / 8 oz / 1 cup butter, softened

225 g / 8 oz / 1 cup caster (superfine) sugar

4 large eggs, beaten

125 g / 4 ½ oz / ¾ cup self-raising flour

100 g / 3 ½ oz / 1 cup ground pecan nuts

100 g / 3 ½ oz dark chocolate (minimum 60% cocoa solids), chopped

FOR THE CHOCOLATE TOPPING

100 g / 3 ½ oz dark chocolate (minimum 60% cocoa solids), chopped

28 g / 1 oz butter

2 tbsp golden syrup

55 g / 2 oz / ½ cup pecan nuts, chopped

METHOD

- Preheat the oven to 180°C (160°C fan) / 355F / gas 4 and butter a bundt tin.

- Cream the butter and sugar together until well whipped, then gradually whisk in the eggs, beating well after each addition.

- Fold in the flour, ground pecans and chocolate chunks, then scrape the mixture into the tin.

- Bake the cake for 45 minutes or until a skewer inserted in the centre comes out clean. Turn the cake out onto a wire rack and leave to cool.

- For the topping, melt the chocolate, butter and syrup together over a low heat, stirring regularly, then spoon it over the cooled cake. Sprinkle with chopped pecan nuts.

TOP TIP
Instead of pecans use chopped pistachios for a different nutty aroma.

Chocolate Layer Cake

SERVES 10–12

PREPARATION TIME 10 MINUTES

COOKING TIME 30–35 MINUTES

INGREDIENTS

225 g / 8 oz / 1 ½ cups self-raising flour

55 g / 2 oz / ½ cup unsweetened cocoa powder

3 tsp baking powder

225 g / 8 oz / 1 cup caster (superfine) sugar

225 g / 8 oz / 1 cup butter

4 large eggs

FOR THE GANACHE

300 ml / 10 ½ fl. oz / 1 ¼ cups double (heavy) cream

300 g / 10 ½ oz dark chocolate (minimum 60% cocoa solids), chopped

75 g / 2 ½ oz / ⅓ cup butter, cubed

METHOD

- Preheat the oven to 180°C (160°C fan) / 355F / gas 4 and grease and line three 20 cm (8 in) round cake tins.

- Whisk together all of the cake ingredients until well whipped.

- Divide the mixture between the tins and bake for 30–35 minutes. The cakes are ready when a toothpick inserted in the centre comes out clean.

- Transfer the cakes to a wire rack to cool completely.

- Bring the cream almost to a simmer, then pour it over the chopped chocolate and stir until smooth.

- Add the butter and blend it in with a stick blender.

- When the ganache has cooled to a spreadable consistency, use it to sandwich the cakes together, finishing with a thick layer on top.

TOP TIP

Add 2 tbsp of espresso to the batter and 1 tbsp of coffee extract to the ganache.

Chocolate Sponge with Apricots

MAKES 12

PREPARATION TIME 10 MINUTES

COOKING TIME 30–35 MINUTES

INGREDIENTS

150 g / 6 oz / 1 cup self-raising flour

28 g / 1 oz / ¼ cup unsweetened
    cocoa powder

2 tsp baking powder

175 g / 6 oz / ¾ cup caster (superfine) sugar

175 g / 6 oz / ¾ cup butter

3 eggs

TO DECORATE

300 ml / 10 ½ fl. oz / 1 ¼ cups double (heavy)
    cream

1 can apricot slices, drained

METHOD

- Preheat the oven to 180°C (160°C fan) / 355F / gas 4 and grease and line two 20 cm (8 in) round cake tins.

- Put all of the cake ingredients in a large mixing bowl and whisk them together until pale and well whipped.

- Divide the mixture between the tins and level the top with a palette knife.

- Bake for 30–35 minutes. The cakes are ready when a toothpick inserted in the centre comes out clean. Transfer the cakes to a wire rack to cool completely.

- Whip the double cream until thick and spoon half of it onto the first cake. Top with two thirds of the apricot slices then position the second cake on top.

- Spread the rest of the cream over the top of the cake and decorate with the remaining apricot slices.

TOP TIP

This recipe would work equally well with raspberries.

Chocolate and Strawberry Gateau

SERVES 10–12

PREPARATION TIME 10 MINUTES

COOKING TIME 45–50 MINUTES

INGREDIENTS

150 g / 6 oz / 1 cup self-raising flour

28 g / 1 oz / ¼ cup cocoa powder

2 tsp baking powder

175 g / 6 oz / ¾ cup caster (superfine) sugar

175 g / 6 oz / ¾ cup butter

3 eggs

TO DECORATE

400 ml / 14 fl. oz / 1 ⅔ cups double (heavy) cream

100 g / 3 ½ oz milk chocolate, chopped

300 g / 10 ½ oz / 2 cups strawberries, sliced

milk chocolate curls, to decorate

METHOD

- Preheat the oven to 180°C (160°C fan) / 355F / gas 4 and grease and line two 20 cm (8 in) round cake tins.

- Whisk together all of the cake ingredients. Divide the mix between the tins and bake for 30–35 minutes.

- The cakes are ready when a toothpick inserted in the centre comes out clean. Transfer the cakes to a wire rack to cool completely.

- Measure one quarter of the cream into a saucepan and bring to a simmer. Pour it over the chopped chocolate and stir until completely smooth.

- Whip the rest of the cream until thick. Fold two thirds of the strawberry slices into the cream and use the strawberry cream to sandwich the two cakes together.

- Pour the slightly cooled chocolate glaze over the cakes and spread it round the sides with a palette knife.

- Put the cake in the fridge for 1 hour to set before decorating with the reserved strawberries and chocolate curls.

TOP TIP

Substitute the strawberries for the same quantity of raspberries.

Chocolate Cake and Plum Terrine

SERVES 8

PREPARATION TIME 2 HOURS 30 MINUTES

COOKING TIME 45 MINUTES

INGREDIENTS

225 g / 8 oz / 1 cup butter, softened

225 g / 8 oz / 1 cup caster (superfine) sugar

4 large eggs, beaten

225 g / 8 oz / 1 ½ cups self-raising flour

1 tbsp unsweetened cocoa powder

75 g / 2 ½ oz dark chocolate, melted

FOR THE FILLING

400 ml / 14 fl. oz / 1 ⅔ cups double (heavy) cream

8 ripe plums, stoned and sliced

METHOD

- Preheat the oven to 180°C (160°C fan) / 355F / gas 4 and grease and line a large loaf tin with greaseproof paper.

- Cream the butter and sugar together until well whipped, then gradually whisk in the eggs, beating well after each addition.

- Sift over and fold in the flour and cocoa powder, then fold in the melted chocolate. Scrape the mixture into the tin and bake for 45 minutes or until a skewer inserted in the centre comes out clean.

- Turn the loaf out onto a wire rack and leave to cool.

- Line the tin with cling film. Slice the cake horizontally into 3 even layers and put the top one back into the tin.

- Whip the cream until thick and spoon half of it into the tin. Top with half of the plums then lay the middle cake layer on top and press down.

- Spoon over the rest of the cream and top with the remaining plum slices before adding the final cake layer.

- Refrigerate for 2 hours to firm up. Turn out of the tin and cut into 8 slices to serve.

TOP TIP

Stir 2 tbsp plum brandy into the filling for a decadent treat.

Dark and White Chocolate Layer Cake

SERVES 8

PREPARATION TIME 45 MINUTES

COOKING TIME 15–20 MINUTES

INGREDIENTS

FOR THE DARK CHOCOLATE CAKE LAYER

100 g / 3 ½ oz / ⅔ cup self-raising flour
28 g / 1 oz / ¼ cup cocoa powder
1 tsp baking powder
100 g / 3 ½ oz / ½ cup caster (superfine) sugar
100 g / 3 ½ oz / ½ cup butter
2 large eggs

FOR THE PLAIN CAKE LAYER

100 g / 3 ½ oz / ⅔ cup self-raising flour
1 tsp baking powder
100 g / 3 ½ oz / ½ cup caster (superfine) sugar
100 g / 3 ½ oz / ½ cup butter
2 large eggs

FOR THE WHITE CHOCOLATE GANACHE

225 g / 8 oz white chocolate
225 ml / 8 fl. oz / 1 cup double (heavy) cream

METHOD

- Preheat the oven to 180°C (160°C fan) / 355F / gas 4 and grease and line two Swiss roll tins.

- Put all of the chocolate cake ingredients in a large mixing bowl and whisk them together until pale and well whipped.

- Spoon the mixture into one of the tins and spread into an even layer with a palette knife. Bake for 15–20 minutes or until springy to the touch.

- Make the plain cake layer using the same method.

- To make the white chocolate ganache, chop the chocolate and transfer to a mixing bowl.

- Heat the cream until it starts to simmer, then pour over the chopped chocolate and stir until the mixture has cooled and thickened.

- Cut the two cakes into thirds and sandwich alternate layers together with the white chocolate ganache.

TOP TIP
Why not also include a dark chocolate ganache for a richer taste?

Toffee Sponge Cake

SERVES 12

PREPARATION TIME 20 MINUTES

COOKING TIME 45–50 MINUTES

INGREDIENTS

150 g / 5 ½ oz / 1 cup self-raising flour
150 g / 5 ½ oz / ¾ cup muscovado sugar
150 g / 5 ½ oz / ⅔ cup butter
3 large eggs
1 tsp baking powder
1 tsp vanilla extract

FOR THE TOFFEE SAUCE

100 g / 3 ½ oz / ½ cup butter
100 g / 3 ½ oz / ½ cup muscovado sugar
100 g / 3 ½ oz / ⅓ cup golden syrup

METHOD

- Preheat the oven to 180°C (160°C fan) / 355F / gas 4 and grease and line a deep 20 cm (8 in) round loose-bottomed cake tin.

- Put all of the cake ingredients in a large mixing bowl and whisk them together until pale and well whipped.

- Scrape the mixture into the tin and level the top with a spatula.

- Bake for 45–50 minutes. The cake is ready when a toothpick inserted in the centre comes out clean.

- Meanwhile, put the toffee sauce ingredients in a small saucepan and stir over a low heat until the butter melts and the sugar dissolves.

- Bring the toffee sauce to the boil, then take it off the heat.

- When the cake comes out of the oven, prick the top with a skewer and spoon over half of the toffee sauce.

- Allow the cake to cool for at least 15 minutes, then cut into wedges and serve the rest of the sauce alongside.

TOP TIP
Add diced cooking apple to the batter for a fruity kick.

Coffee and Almond Sponge

SERVES 10

PREPARATION TIME 10 MINUTES

COOKING TIME 35–40 MINUTES

INGREDIENTS

200 g / 7 oz / 1 ⅓ cups self-raising flour

200 g / 7 oz / ¾ cup caster (superfine) sugar

200 g / 7 oz / ¾ cup butter

4 eggs

1 tsp baking powder

1 tbsp instant espresso powder

TO DECORATE

200 g / 7 oz / ¾ cup butter, softened

400 g / 14 oz / 4 cups icing (confectioners') sugar

1 tbsp instant espresso powder

100 g / 3 ½ oz / 1 ⅓ cups flaked (slivered) almonds, toasted

6 chocolate-coated coffee beans

METHOD

- Preheat the oven to 180°C (160°C fan) / 355F / gas 4 and grease and line two 20 cm (8 in) round loose-bottomed cake tins.

- Put all of the cake ingredients in a large mixing bowl. Whisk them together until pale and well whipped.

- Divide the mixture between the 2 tins and bake for 35–40 minutes. The cakes are ready when a toothpick inserted in the centre comes out clean.

- Transfer the cakes to a wire rack to cool completely.

- To make the buttercream, whisk the butter, then gradually add the icing sugar and espresso powder. Whisk until smooth and well whipped. If the mixture is too stiff add 1 tsp of warm water.

- Use half of the buttercream to sandwich the two cakes together and spread the rest over the top and sides with a palette knife. Draw lines across the top of the cake with the back of a fork.

- Press the almonds onto the side of the cake with your hands and decorate the top with coffee beans.

TOP TIP

Use the same quantity of matcha powder as you would espresso coffee for a delicate cake.

Coffee Cinnamon Cake

SERVES 8–10

PREPARATION TIME 30 MINUTES

COOKING TIME 30 MINUTES

INGREDIENTS

120 g / 4 oz / ½ cup self-raising flour

1 tsp baking powder

120 g / 4 oz / ½ cup butter, softened

120 g / 4 oz / ½ cup caster (superfine) sugar

90 g / 3 oz / ½ cup mixed nuts, chopped

2 eggs

1 tbsp instant coffee mixed with
    1 tbsp hot water

1 tsp ground cinnamon

FOR THE FILLING AND ICING

100 g / 3 ½ oz / ½ cup butter, softened

225 g / 8 oz / 1 cup icing (confectioners')
    sugar

2 tbsp instant coffee dissolved in
    1 tbsp hot water

¼ tsp ground cinnamon

METHOD

- Preheat the oven to 170°C (150°C fan) / 325F / gas 3. Grease and line two 18 cm (7 in) cake tins.

- Sieve the flour and baking powder into a large bowl, then add the other ingredients and whisk until completely combined.

- Divide the mixture equally between the two cake tins, then top with the nuts and cook for 30 minutes.

- Remove from the tins and cool on a wire rack.

- To make the icing, cream the butter and sugar together, then stir in the coffee. Refrigerate until needed.

- Use the icing to sandwich the cakes together, then smooth the remainder over the top and sides with a palette knife. Dust with a little cinnamon.

TOP TIP

Lightly pulse walnuts in a blender and sprinkle over the top.

33

Tea and Almond Cake

SERVES 8

PREPARATION TIME 15 MINUTES

COOKING TIME 55 MINUTES

INGREDIENTS

225 g / 8 oz / 1 ½ cups self-raising flour

100 g / 3 ½ oz / ½ cup butter, cubed

100 g / 3 ½ oz / ½ cup caster (superfine) sugar

150 g / 5 ½ oz / 2 cups flaked (slivered) almonds

3 tbsp loose leaf tea

1 large egg

75 ml / 2 ½ fl. oz / ⅓ cup strongly brewed tea, cold

METHOD

- Preheat the oven to 180°C (160°C fan) / 355F / gas 4 and line a 23 cm (9 in) round cake tin with non-stick baking paper.

- Sieve the flour into a mixing bowl and rub in the butter until it resembles fine breadcrumbs. Stir in the sugar, reserving 2 tbsp.

- Mix the slivered almonds and tea leaves with the rest of the sugar, then add half of the mixture to the bowl.

- Lightly beat the egg with the tea and stir it into the dry ingredients until combined.

- Scrape the mixture into the tin and scatter the rest of the almond mixture on top.

- Bake for 55 minutes or until a skewer inserted in the centre comes out clean.

- Transfer the cake to a wire rack and leave to cool completely.

TOP TIP

Replace the slivered almonds with chopped hazelnuts (cobnuts).

Almond and Honey Cake

SERVES 8

PREPARATION TIME 25 MINUTES

COOKING TIME 35–40 MINUTES

INGREDIENTS

55 g / 2 oz / / ⅓ cup self-raising flour, sifted

55 g / 2 oz / ½ cup ground almonds

55 g / 2 oz / ½ cup caster (superfine) sugar

110 g / 4 oz / ⅓ cup honey

110 g / 4 oz / ½ cup butter, softened

2 large eggs

1 tsp almond essence

FOR THE TOPPING

4 tbsp runny honey

60 g / 2 oz / 1 cup flaked (slivered) almonds

METHOD

- Preheat the oven to 190°C (170°C fan) / gas 5 and grease and line a 23 cm (9 in) round cake tin.

- Combine the cake ingredients in a bowl and whisk together until smooth.

- Scrape the mixture into the prepared tin and bake for 30–35 minutes. Test with a wooden toothpick and if it comes out clean, the cake is done.

- Mix the honey and almonds together and spoon the mixture on top of the cake.

- Return the cake to the oven for 5 minutes or until the honey melts into the cake and the almonds turn golden.

- Transfer the cake to a wire rack to cool.

TOP TIP
Add 1 tsp of orange blossom to the batter instead of the almond essence.

Orange, Almond and Cardamom Sponge

SERVES 10–12

PREPARATION TIME 30 MINUTES

COOKING TIME 45–50 MINUTES

INGREDIENTS

150 g / 6 oz / 1 cup stoneground
wholemeal flour
1 tsp baking powder
28 g / 1 oz / ¼ cup ground almonds
28 g / 1 oz / ¼ cup blanched almonds,
finely chopped
2 tsp baking powder
175 g / 6 oz / ¾ cup caster (superfine) sugar
175 g / 6 oz / ¾ cup butter
3 large eggs
1 orange, zest finely grated

FOR THE CRÈME PATISSERIE

4 large egg yolks
75 g / 2 ½ oz / ⅓ cup caster (superfine) sugar
1 tsp vanilla extract
2 tsp cornflour (cornstarch)
450 ml / 16 fl. oz / 1 ¾ cups whole milk
4 cardamom pods, crushed
icing (confectioners') sugar to dust

METHOD

- Preheat the oven to 180°C (160°C fan) / 355F / gas 4 and grease and line a deep 20 cm (8 in) round cake tin.

- Whisk together all of the cake ingredients until well whipped.

- Scrape the mixture into the tin and bake for 45–50 minutes. The cake is ready when a toothpick inserted in the centre comes out clean.

- Transfer the cake to a wire rack to cool completely, then cut in half horizontally.

- To make the crème patisserie, whisk together the egg yolks, sugar, vanilla extract and cornflour.

- Heat the milk and cardamom almost to a simmer, then strain it through a sieve and gradually whisk it into the egg mixture.

- Scrape the custard back into the saucepan and cook over a medium heat until it thickens, stirring constantly.

- Pour it into a bowl and leave to cool to room temperature.

- Beat the crème patisserie until smooth and use it to sandwich the cake back together. Dust with icing sugar before serving.

TOP TIP

A vanilla sponge also works well — replace the orange zest with 1 tsp vanilla essence.

Orange Drizzle Cake

SERVES 10

PREPARATION TIME 10 MINUTES

COOKING TIME 35–40 MINUTES

INGREDIENTS

150 g / 5 ½ oz / 1 cup self-raising flour

150 g / 5 ½ oz / ⅔ cup caster (superfine) sugar

150 g / 5 ½ oz / ⅔ cup butter

3 eggs

1 tsp baking powder

1 tbsp orange zest

2 tbsp orange juice

FOR THE DRIZZLE

100 g / 3 ½ oz / ½ cup caster (superfine) sugar

50 ml / 1 ¾ fl. oz / ¼ cup orange juice

METHOD

- Preheat the oven to 180°C (160°C fan) / 355F / gas 4 and grease and line a 20 cm (8 in) round cake tin.

- Put all of the cake ingredients in a large mixing bowl. Whisk them together until pale and well whipped.

- Scrape the mixture into the tin and level the top with a spatula.

- Bake for 35–40 minutes. The cake is ready when a toothpick inserted in the centre comes out clean.

- While the cake is cooking, stir the caster sugar with the orange juice until the sugar has dissolved.

- When the cake comes out of the oven, spoon the orange drizzle all over the surface and leave it to cool in the tin, before removing and serving.

TOP TIP
For a sharper but delicious tasting cake swap the orange juice and zest for lemon.

Apple and Cinnamon Cake

SERVES 8

PREPARATION TIME 15 MINUTES

COOKING TIME 55 MINUTES

INGREDIENTS

225 g / 8 oz / 1 ½ cups self-raising flour
1 tsp ground cinnamon
100 g / 3 ½ oz / ½ cup butter, cubed
100 g / 3 ½ oz / ½ cup caster (superfine) sugar
1 large egg
75 ml / 2 ½ fl. oz / ⅓ cup whole (full-fat) milk
2 apples, peeled and grated

FOR THE TOPPING

100 g / 3 ½ oz / ½ cup cream cheese
4 tbsp golden syrup
1 tsp ground cinnamon

METHOD

- Preheat the oven to 180°C (160°C fan) / 355F / gas 4 and grease and line a 23 cm (9 in) round cake tin.

- Sieve the flour and cinnamon into a mixing bowl and rub in the butter until it resembles fine breadcrumbs, then stir in the sugar.

- Lightly beat the egg with the milk and grated apple and stir it into the dry ingredients until just combined.

- Scrape the mixture into the cake tin and bake for 55 minutes or until a skewer inserted comes out clean.

- Transfer the cake to a wire rack and leave to cool completely.

- Spread the top of the cake with cream cheese, swirling it with the back of the spoon.

- Heat the golden syrup with the cinnamon until runny, then spoon it all over the cake to glaze.

TOP TIP

Serve with a dollop of crème fraiche on the side.

Pineapple Upside-down Cake

SERVES 8

PREPARATION TIME 15 MINUTES

COOKING TIME 35 MINUTES

INGREDIENTS

300 g / 10 ½ oz / 2 cups self-raising flour

2 tsp baking powder

250 g / 9 oz / 1 ¼ cups caster (superfine) sugar

250 g / 9 oz / 1 ¼ cups butter, softened

5 large eggs

4 tbsp raspberry jam (jelly)

4 canned pineapple rings, drained

METHOD

- Preheat the oven to 170°C (150°C fan) / 340F / gas 3 and butter a 23 cm (9 in) round cake tin.

- Sieve the flour and baking powder into a mixing bowl and add the sugar, butter and eggs. Beat the mixture until smooth and well whipped.

- Spread the jam over the base of the cake tin and arrange the pineapple rings on top.

- Spoon in the cake mixture and bake for 35 minutes or until a skewer inserted in the centre comes out clean.

- Leave the cake to cool for 20 minutes before turning out onto a serving plate.

TOP TIP

Try 3 ripe bananas sliced into ½ cm thickness instead of the pineapple.

45

Pear Cake

SERVES 6–8
PREPARATION TIME 20 MINUTES
COOKING TIME 1 HOUR

INGREDIENTS

200 g / 7 oz / ¾ cup butter, softened

100 g / 3 ½ oz / ½ cup caster (superfine) sugar

100 g / 3 ½ oz / ½ cup soft dark brown sugar

2 eggs, beaten

1 tsp vanilla extract

½ tsp ground cinnamon

200 g / 7 oz / ¾ cup self-raising flour

½ tsp baking powder

a pinch of salt

2–3 ripe pears, peeled cored and chopped

METHOD

- Preheat the oven to 160°C (140°C fan) / 310F / gas 3. Grease and line a large deep loaf tin.

- Beat the butter and sugar together, then whisk in the eggs a little at a time, beating thoroughly after each addition. Stir in the vanilla extract and cinnamon.

- Using a metal spoon, fold in the flour, baking powder and salt. Stir in the pears.

- Pour into the loaf tin, ensuring the pears are evenly distributed, and bake for 1 hour or until an inserted skewer comes out clean.

- Leave to cool in the tin before turning out onto a wire rack to cool completely.

TOP TIP
The same quantity of chopped apple will give a similar result.

Peach Cake with Lemon Thyme Sugar

SERVES 8

PREPARATION TIME 15 MINUTES

COOKING TIME 55 MINUTES

INGREDIENTS

225 g / 8 oz / 1 ½ cups self-raising flour
100 g / 3 ½ oz / ½ cup butter, cubed
100 g / 3 ½ oz / ½ cup caster (superfine) sugar
1 large egg
75 ml / 2 ½ fl. oz / ⅓ cup whole milk
4 peaches, halved and stoned

FOR THE LEMON THYME SUGAR

1 tbsp lemon thyme leaves
60 g / 2 oz / ¼ cup caster (superfine) sugar

METHOD

- Preheat the oven to 180°C (160°C fan) / 355F / gas 4 and butter a round deep baking dish.

- To make the lemon thyme sugar, bruise the thyme leaves with a mortar and pestle, then add half the sugar and pound again. Stir in the rest of the sugar and set aside.

- Sieve the flour into a mixing bowl and rub in the butter until it resembles fine breadcrumbs, then stir in the sugar.

- Lightly beat the egg with the milk and stir it into the dry ingredients until just combined.

- Scrape the mixture into the baking dish and level the surface then press in the peach halves, cut side up.

- Bake the cake for 55 minutes or until a skewer inserted in the centre comes out clean.

- Transfer the cake to a wire rack and sprinkle with the lemon thyme sugar, then leave to cool completely.

TOP TIP

Replace the lemon thyme with 1 tbsp of edible lavender flowers.

Strawberry Jam Swiss Roll

SERVES 8

PREPARATION TIME 30 MINUTES

COOKING TIME 10 MINUTES

INGREDIENTS

3 eggs

75 g / 2 ½ oz / ⅓ cup caster (superfine) sugar

60 g / 2 oz / ¼ cup plain (all-purpose) flour

200 g / 7 oz / ¾ cup strawberry jam (jelly)

METHOD

- Preheat the oven to 180°C (160°C fan) / 350F / gas 5. Grease and line a 23cm (9 in) swiss roll tin or shallow baking tray.

- Whisk the eggs and sugar together until pale and tripled in volume.

- Sieve the flour into a bowl, then fold into the egg mixture a little at a time until thoroughly combined.

- Pour into the swiss roll tin and bake for 10 minutes until springy.

- Place a large piece of baking parchment on a work surface and sprinkle with a little sugar. Turn the cake out onto the baking parchment at one end, removing the lining paper from the tin.

- Trim the edges of the sponge to neaten, then spread with a layer of jam. Roll up from the short end to make a fat sausage shape while still warm.

- Leave to cool, then slice as required.

TOP TIP
Use raspberry jam (jelly) in place of the strawberry jam (jelly).

Carrot Layer Cake

SERVES 8–10

PREPARATION TIME 25 MINUTES

COOKING TIME 30–35 MINUTES

INGREDIENTS

175 g / 6 oz / 1 cup light brown sugar
2 large eggs
150 ml / 5 fl. oz / ⅔ cup sunflower oil
175 g / 6 oz / 1 ¼ cup stoneground
    wholemeal flour
3 tsp baking powder
2 tsp ground cinnamon
1 orange, zest finely grated
200 g / 7 oz / 1 ⅔ cup carrots, washed and
    coarsely grated

FOR THE ICING

225 g / 8 oz / 1 cup cream cheese
110 g / 4 oz / ½ cup butter, softened
225 g / 8 oz / 2 ¼ cups icing
    (confectioners') sugar
1 tsp vanilla extract
½ tsp nutmeg freshly grated

METHOD

- Preheat the oven to 190°C (170°C fan) / 375F / gas 5 and line two 20 cm (8 in) round cake tins with greaseproof paper.

- Whisk the sugar, eggs and oil together for 3 minutes until thick.

- Fold in the flour, baking powder and cinnamon, followed by the orange zest and carrots.

- Divide the mixture between the tins and bake for 30–35 minutes.

- Test with a wooden toothpick, if it comes out clean, the cakes are done. Transfer the cakes to a wire rack and leave to cool.

- To make the icing, beat the cream cheese and butter together with a wooden spoon until light and fluffy, then beat in the icing sugar a quarter at a time.

- Add the vanilla extract, then use a whisk to whip the mixture for 2 minutes or until smooth and light.

- Use half of the icing to sandwich the cakes together and spread the rest over the top of the cake with a palette knife. Grate over a little nutmeg to finish.

TOP TIP

Mascarpone makes a good replacement for the cream cheese in the icing.

Carrot and Walnut Cake

SERVES 8–10

PREPARATION TIME 25 MINUTES

COOKING TIME 30–35 MINUTES

INGREDIENTS

175 g / 6 oz / 1 cup soft light brown sugar

2 large eggs

150 ml / 5 fl. oz / ⅔ cup sunflower oil

175 g / 6 oz / 1 ¼ cups stoneground
    wholemeal flour

3 tsp baking powder

2 tsp ground cinnamon

1 orange, zest finely grated

200 g / 7 oz / 1 ⅔ cups carrots, washed and
    coarsely grated

100 g / 3 ½ oz / ¾ cup walnuts, chopped

FOR THE ICING

225 g / 8 oz / 1 cup cream cheese

110 g / 4 oz / ½ cup butter, softened

225 g / 8 oz / 2 ¼ cups icing
    (confectioners') sugar

1 tsp vanilla extract

METHOD

- Preheat the oven to 190°C (170°C fan) / 375F / gas 5 and line two 20 cm (8 in) round cake tins with greaseproof paper.

- Whisk the sugar, eggs and oil together until thick.

- Fold in the flour, baking powder and cinnamon, followed by the orange zest, carrots and walnuts.

- Divide the mixture between the tins and bake for 30–35 minutes.

- Transfer the cakes to a wire rack and leave to cool.

- To make the icing, beat the cream cheese and butter together with a wooden spoon until light and fluffy, then beat in the icing sugar a quarter at a time.

- Add the vanilla extract, then whisk the mixture until smooth and light.

- Use a third of the icing to sandwich the cakes together and spread the rest over the top and sides.

TOP TIP

Replace the walnuts with roughly chopped hazelnuts (cobnuts).

Coconut Cake with Redcurrant Compote

SERVES 8–10

PREPARATION TIME 5 MINUTES

COOKING TIME 45–55 MINUTES

INGREDIENTS

225 g / 8 oz / 1 cup butter, softened

225 g / 8 oz / 1 cup caster (superfine) sugar

4 large eggs, beaten

225 g / 4 ½ oz / 1 ½ cups self-raising flour

100 g / 3 ½ oz / 1 cup desiccated coconut

FOR THE COMPOTE

100 g / 3 ½ oz / ⅔ cup redcurrants

4 tbsp caster (superfine) sugar

METHOD

- Preheat the oven to 180°C (160°C fan) / 355F / gas 4 and grease and line a 23 cm (9 in) round cake tin with greaseproof paper.

- Cream the butter and sugar together, then gradually whisk in the eggs, beating well after each addition.

- Fold in the flour and coconut, then scrape the mixture into the tin.

- Bake the cake for 45–55 minutes or until a skewer inserted in the centre comes out clean.

- Meanwhile, put the redcurrants in a small saucepan with the sugar. Cover and cook gently for 5 minutes, then remove the lid, give the mixture a stir and cook for a few more minutes until the redcurrants start to burst and the juices thicken.

- Leave the cake to cool for 20 minutes before serving warm with the compote spooned over the top.

TOP TIP

Replace redcurrants with gooseberries for a different fruity kick.

Gluten-free Coconut Cake

SERVES 8–10

PREPARATION TIME 5 MINUTES

COOKING TIME 45–55 MINUTES

INGREDIENTS

225 g / 8 oz / 1 cup butter, softened

225 g / 8 oz / 1 cup caster (superfine) sugar

1 vanilla pod, seeds only

4 large eggs, beaten

225 g / 4 ½ oz / 1 ½ cups rice flour

1 tsp baking powder

100 g / 3 ½ oz / 1 cup desiccated coconut

METHOD

- Preheat the oven to 180°C (160°C fan) / 355F / gas 4 and grease and line a 23 cm (9 in) round cake tin with greaseproof paper.

- Cream the butter, sugar and vanilla seeds together until well whipped, then gradually whisk in the eggs, beating well after each addition.

- Fold in the flour, baking powder and coconut, then scrape the mixture into a cake tin.

- Bake the cake for 45–55 minutes or until a skewer inserted in the centre comes out clean.

TOP TIP

Replace the coconut with ground almonds and top with flaked (slivered) almonds.

Loaf Cakes

Pound Cake

SERVES 8

PREPARATION TIME 5 MINUTES

COOKING TIME 45–55 MINUTES

INGREDIENTS

150 g / 1 lb / 2 cups butter, softened

450 g / 1 lb / 2 cups caster (superfine) sugar

8 large eggs, beaten

450 g / 1 lb / 3 cups self-raising flour

METHOD

- Preheat the oven to 180°C (160°C fan) / 355F / gas 4 and grease and line a 4 lb loaf tin, or 2 x 2 lb loaf tins, with greaseproof paper.

- Cream the butter and sugar together until well whipped, then gradually whisk in the eggs, beating well after each addition.

- Fold in the flour then scrape the mixture into the tin.

- Bake the cake for 45–55 minutes or until a skewer inserted in the centre comes out clean.

- Turn the loaf out onto a wire rack and leave to cool before slicing.

TOP TIP

For a fruitier taste, stir in 110 g / 4 oz raisins when you fold in the flour.

Lemon and Poppy Seed Loaf Cake

SERVES 8

PREPARATION TIME 10 MINUTES

COOKING TIME 35–40 MINUTES

INGREDIENTS

150 g / 5 ½ oz / 1 cup self-raising flour

150 g / 5 ½ oz / ⅔ cup caster (superfine) sugar

150 g / 5 ½ oz / ⅔ cup butter

3 eggs

1 tsp baking powder

1 tbsp lemon zest

2 tbsp lemon juice

2 tbsp poppy seeds

TO DECORATE

candied lemon peel, thinly sliced

METHOD

- Preheat the oven to 180°C (160°C fan) / 355F / gas 4 and grease and line a small loaf tin.

- Put all of the cake ingredients in a large mixing bowl and whisk them together until pale and well whipped.

- Scrape the mixture into the tin and level the top with a spatula.

- Bake for 35–40 minutes. The cake is ready when a toothpick inserted in the centre comes out clean.

- Transfer the cake to a wire rack to cool completely before garnishing with the candied lemon peel.

TOP TIP

Mix 1 tbsp of orange with the lemon juice and add 1 tbsp of orange zest to the batter.

Iced Lemon Loaf Cake

SERVES 10

PREPARATION TIME 20 MINUTES

COOKING TIME 35–40 MINUTES

INGREDIENTS

150 g / 5 ½ oz / 1 cup self-raising flour
150 g / 5 ½ oz / ⅔ cup caster (superfine) sugar
150 g / 5 ½ oz / ⅔ cup butter
3 eggs
1 tsp baking powder
1 tbsp lemon zest
2 tbsp lemon juice

TO DECORATE

200 g / 7 oz / 2 cups icing (confectioners')
    sugar
1–2 tbsp lemon juice
1 lemon, sliced

METHOD

- Preheat the oven to 180°C (160°C fan) / 355F / gas 4 and grease and line a small loaf tin.

- Put all of the cake ingredients in a large mixing bowl. Whisk them together until pale and well whipped.

- Scrape the mixture into the tin and level the top with a spatula.

- Bake for 35–40 minutes. The cake is ready when a toothpick inserted in the centre comes out clean.

- Transfer the cake to a wire rack to cool completely.

- Sieve the icing sugar and stir in just enough lemon juice to produce a thick but pourable icing.

- Pour the icing all over the cake and allow it to drip down the sides. Garnish with twisted lemon slices.

TOP TIP
Add 2 tbsp of edible lavender flowers to the batter.

Banana and Walnut Loaf Cake

SERVES 8

PREPARATION TIME 10 MINUTES

COOKING TIME 55 MINUTES

INGREDIENTS

3 very ripe bananas

110 g / 4 oz / ½ cup soft light brown sugar

2 large eggs

120 ml / 4 fl. oz / ½ cup sunflower oil

225 g / 8 oz / 1 ½ cup plain
    (all-purpose) flour

1 tsp bicarbonate of (baking) soda

75 g / 2 ½ oz / ⅔ cup walnuts, chopped

METHOD

- Preheat the oven to 170°C (150°C fan) / 340F / gas 3 and line a long thin loaf tin with non-stick baking paper.

- Mash the bananas roughly with a fork, then whisk in the sugar, eggs and oil.

- Sieve the flour and bicarbonate of soda into the bowl and add the chopped walnuts. Stir just enough to evenly mix all the ingredients together.

- Scrape the mixture into the loaf tin and bake for 55 minutes or until a skewer inserted in the centre comes out clean.

- Transfer the cake to a wire rack and leave to cool completely.

TOP TIP

Use the same quantity of chopped hazelnuts (cobnuts) instead of the walnuts.

Banana and Chocolate Chip Loaf Cake

SERVES 8

PREPARATION TIME 10 MINUTES

COOKING TIME 55 MINUTES

INGREDIENTS

3 very ripe bananas

110 g / 4 oz / ⅓ cup dark brown sugar

2 large eggs

120 ml / 4 fl. oz / ½ cup sunflower oil

225 g / 8 oz / 1 ½ cup plain (all-purpose) flour

1 tsp bicarbonate of (baking) soda

75 g / 2 ½ oz / ½ cup chocolate chips

METHOD

- Preheat the oven to 170°C (150°C fan) / 340F / gas 3 and line a loaf tin with non-stick baking paper.

- Mash the bananas roughly with a fork, then whisk in the sugar, eggs and oil.

- Sieve the flour and bicarbonate of soda into the bowl and add the chocolate chips. Stir just enough to evenly mix all the ingredients together.

- Scrape the mixture into the loaf tin and bake for 55 minutes or until a skewer inserted in the centre comes out clean.

- Transfer the cake to a wire rack and leave to cool completely.

TOP TIP
Use fudge squares instead of chocolate chips for a more toffee-like taste.

Banana and Hazelnut Loaf Cake

SERVES 8

PREPARATION TIME 10 MINUTES

COOKING TIME 55 MINUTES

INGREDIENTS

3 very ripe bananas

110 g / 4 oz / ½ cup soft light brown sugar

2 large eggs

120 ml / 4 fl. oz / ½ cup sunflower oil

125 g / 4 ½ oz / ¾ cup plain (all-purpose) flour

2 tsp baking powder

100 g / 3 ½ oz / 1 cup ground hazelnuts (cobnuts)

METHOD

- Preheat the oven to 170°C (150°C fan) / 340F / gas 3 and line a long thin loaf tin with non-stick baking paper.

- Mash the bananas roughly with a fork then whisk in the sugar, eggs and oil.

- Sieve the flour and baking powder into the bowl and add the ground hazelnuts. Stir just enough to evenly mix all the ingredients together.

- Scrape the mixture into the loaf tin and bake for 55 minutes or until a skewer inserted in the centre comes out clean.

- Transfer the cake to a wire rack and leave to cool completely.

TOP TIP

Substitute the hazelnuts with 100 g / 3 ½ oz of chopped toasted pine nuts.

Apple and Poppy Seed Cake

SERVES 8

PREPARATION TIME 15 MINUTES

COOKING TIME 45 MINUTES

INGREDIENTS

300 g / 10 ½ oz / 2 cups self-raising flour

2 tsp baking powder

250 g / 9 oz / 1 ½ cups dark brown sugar

250 g / 9 oz / 1 ¼ cups butter, softened

5 large eggs

2 tbsp poppy seeds

1 tbsp caster (superfine) sugar

3 eating apples, cored and sliced

METHOD

- Preheat the oven to 170°C (150°C fan) / 340F / gas 3 and butter a round baking dish.

- Sieve the flour and baking powder into a mixing bowl and add the brown sugar, butter, eggs and half the poppy seeds.

- Beat the mixture until smooth and well whipped.

- Sprinkle the rest of the poppy seeds and the caster sugar over the base of the baking dish and arrange the apple slices on top.

- Spoon the cake mixture on top of the apple and bake for 45 minutes or until a skewer inserted in the centre comes out clean.

- Leave the cake to cool for 20 minutes before turning out onto a serving plate.

TOP TIP

Substitute the apples for sliced pears and sprinkle with flaked (slivered) almonds.

Rhubarb Loaf Cake

SERVES 8

PREPARATION TIME 10 MINUTES

COOKING TIME 55 MINUTES

INGREDIENTS

300 g / 10 ½ oz / 2 cups self-raising flour

2 tsp baking powder

250 g / 9 oz / 1 ¼ cups caster (superfine) sugar

250 g / 9 oz / 1 ¼ cups butter, softened

5 large eggs

2 sticks rhubarb, chopped

METHOD

- Preheat the oven to 170°C (150°C fan) / 340F / gas 3 and line a large loaf tin with non-stick baking paper.

- Sieve the flour and baking powder into a mixing bowl and add the sugar, butter and eggs.

- Beat the mixture until smooth and well whipped, then fold in the rhubarb.

- Scrape the mixture into the loaf tin and bake for 55 minutes or until a skewer inserted in the centre comes out clean.

- Transfer the cake to a wire rack and leave to cool completely.

TOP TIP

Add the zest of 1 lemon and 2 tbsp of lemon juice for a citrus kick.

Mini Apricot Loaf Cakes

MAKES 12

PREPARATION TIME 10 MINUTES

COOKING TIME 15–20 MINUTES

INGREDIENTS

110 g / 4 oz / ⅔ cup self-raising flour, sifted

110 g / 4 oz / ½ cup caster (superfine) sugar

110 g / 4 oz / ½ cup butter, softened

2 large eggs

1 tsp vanilla extract

75 g / 2 ½ oz / ⅓ cup dried apricots, chopped

METHOD

- Preheat the oven to 190°C (170°C fan) / 375F / gas 5 and oil a 12-hole silicone mini loaf cake mould.

- Combine the flour, sugar, butter, eggs and vanilla in a bowl and whisk together for 2 minutes or until smooth. Fold in the chopped apricots.

- Divide the mixture between the moulds, then transfer the mould to the oven and bake for 15–20 minutes.

- Test with a wooden toothpick, if it comes out clean, the cakes are done.

- Transfer the cakes to a wire rack and leave to cool completely.

TOP TIP

For a richer and darker loaf cake use chopped dates instead of the apricots.

Chocolate Orange Loaf Cake

SERVES 8

PREPARATION TIME 15 MINUTES

COOKING TIME 45 MINUTES

INGREDIENTS

225 g / 8 oz / 1 cup butter, softened

225 g / 8 oz / 1 cup caster (superfine) sugar

1 orange, zest finely grated

4 large eggs, beaten

225 g / 8 oz / 1 ½ cups self-raising flour

1 tbsp unsweetened cocoa powder

55 g / 1 oz / ⅓ cup candied orange peel

METHOD

- Preheat the oven to 180⁰C (160⁰C fan) / 350F / gas 4 and grease and line a large loaf tin with greaseproof paper.

- Cream together the butter, sugar and orange zest until well whipped, then gradually whisk in the eggs, beating well after each addition.

- Sift over and fold in the flour and cocoa powder.

- Scrape the mixture into the tin and bake for 45 minutes or until a skewer inserted in the centre comes out clean.

- Turn the loaf out onto a wire rack and leave to cool completely before decorating with candied peel.

TOP TIP
Add 2 tbsp of strong coffee or espresso to the mixture for a richer cake.

Chocolate and Hazelnut Mini Loaf Cakes

MAKES 12

PREPARATION TIME 25 MINUTES

COOKING TIME 20–25 MINUTES

INGREDIENTS

1 large egg

120 ml / 4 fl. oz / ½ cup milk

120 ml / 4 fl. oz / ½ cup sunflower oil

375 g / 12 ½ oz / 2 ½ cups self-raising
    flour, sifted

55 g / 2 oz / ½ cup cocoa powder, sifted

1 tsp baking powder

200 g / 7 oz / ¾ cup caster (superfine) sugar

75 g / 2 ½ oz / ⅔ cup hazelnuts
    (cobnuts), chopped

110 g / 4 oz dark chocolate (minimum 60%
    cocoa solids), chopped

METHOD

- Preheat the oven to 180°C (160°C fan)
  / 350F / gas 4 and line 12 mini loaf cake
  tins with cases.

- Beat the egg in a jug with the milk and
  oil until well mixed.

- Mix the flour, cocoa, baking powder,
  sugar, hazelnuts and chocolate in a
  bowl, then pour in the egg mixture
  and stir just enough to combine.

- Divide the mixture between the paper
  cases, then bake in the oven for
  20–25 minutes.

- Test with a wooden toothpick, if it
  comes out clean, the cakes are done.

- Transfer the cakes to a wire rack and
  leave to cool completely.

TOP TIP

Substitute the hazelnuts
(cobnuts) for the
same quantity of
pistachios.

Chocolate Truffle Loaf Cake

SERVES 8–10

PREPARATION TIME 15 MINUTES

COOKING TIME 40–50 MINUTES

INGREDIENTS

600 g / 1 lb 5 oz / 2 ¾ cups cream cheese

150 ml / 5 fl. oz / ⅔ cup sour cream

175 g / 6 oz / ¾ cup caster (superfine) sugar

2 large eggs

1 egg yolk

2 tbsp plain (all-purpose) flour

2 tbsp cocoa powder, plus extra
    for dusting

200 g / 7 oz dark chocolate (minimum 60%
    cocoa solids), melted

METHOD

- Preheat the oven to 180°C (160°C fan) / 355F / gas 4 and grease and line a large loaf tin with greaseproof paper.

- Put all of the ingredients in a bowl and whisk together until smooth.

- Scrape the mixture into the loaf tin and level the top with a palette knife.

- Put the loaf tin in a large roasting tin and pour around enough boiling water to come half way up the side of the loaf tin.

- Bake the cake for 40–50 minutes or until the centre is only just set.

- Leave to cool completely in the tin, then refrigerate for 2 hours before turning out and dusting with cocoa.

TOP TIP

Add 2 tsp of peppermint essence to the truffle mix for a subtle mint taste.

Chocolate Ganache Mini Loaf Cakes

MAKES 12

PREPARATION TIME 20 MINUTES

COOKING TIME 15–20 MINUTES

INGREDIENTS

110 g / 4 oz / ⅔ cup self-raising flour, sifted

110 g / 4 oz / ½ cup caster (superfine) sugar

2 tbsp cocoa powder

110 g / 4 oz / ½ cup butter, softened

2 large eggs

FOR THE GANACHE

100 ml / 3 ½ fl. oz / ½ cup double (heavy) cream

100 g / 3 ½ oz milk chocolate, chopped

1 tbsp butter, softened

METHOD

- Preheat the oven to 190°C (170°C fan) / 375F / gas 5 and oil a 12-hole silicone mini loaf cake mould.

- Combine the flour, sugar, cocoa, butter and eggs in a bowl and whisk together for 2 minutes or until smooth.

- Divide the mixture between the moulds, then transfer the mould to the oven and bake for 15–20 minutes.

- Test with a wooden toothpick, if it comes out clean, the cakes are done.

- Transfer the cakes to a wire rack and leave to cool completely.

- Heat the cream to a simmer, then pour it over the chocolate and stir until smooth.

- Add the butter and blend it in with a stick blender.

- When the ganache has cooled to a spreadable consistency, spread it on top of the cakes with a palette knife.

TOP TIP

Add 3 tbsp of espresso or strong coffee to the ganache mixture for a deeper taste.

Chocolate and Almond Marble Loaf

SERVES 10

PREPARATION TIME 10 MINUTES

COOKING TIME 45–50 MINUTES

INGREDIENTS

100 g / 3 ½ oz / ⅔ cup self-raising flour

1 tsp baking powder

50 g / 1 ¾ oz / ½ cup ground almonds

150 g / 5 ½ oz / ⅔ cup caster (superfine) sugar

150 g / 5 ½ oz / ⅔ cup butter

3 large eggs

2 tbsp cocoa powder

4 tbsp flaked (slivered) almonds

METHOD

- Preheat the oven to 180°C (160°C fan) / 355F / gas 4 and grease and line a loaf tin with greaseproof paper.

- Sieve the flour and baking powder into a mixing bowl, then add the ground almonds, sugar, butter and eggs and whisk until pale and well whipped.

- Divide the mixture into two bowls. Mix the cocoa powder with 2 tbsp hot water until smooth and stir it into one of the bowls.

- Spoon the mixtures into the tin, alternating between chocolate and plain, then draw a knife down the centre to marble.

- Sprinkle with flaked almonds and bake for 45–50 minutes. The cake is ready when a toothpick inserted in the centre comes out clean.

- Transfer the cake to a wire rack to cool completely.

TOP TIP

Use 4 tbsp of roughly chopped pistachios to top the cake before baking.

Chocolate-covered Coconut Loaf Cake

SERVES 8–10

PREPARATION TIME 15 MINUTES

COOKING TIME 45–55 MINUTES

INGREDIENTS

225 g / 8 oz / 1 cup butter, softened

225 g / 8 oz / 1 cup caster (superfine) sugar

4 large eggs, beaten

225 g / 4 ½ oz / 1 ½ cups self-raising flour

100 g / 3 ½ oz / 1 cup desiccated coconut

FOR THE TOPPING

200 g / 7 oz dark chocolate (minimum 60% cocoa solids)

METHOD

- Preheat the oven to 180°C (160°C fan) / 355F / gas 4 and grease and line a loaf tin with greaseproof paper.

- Cream the butter and sugar together until well whipped, then gradually whisk in the eggs, beating well after each addition.

- Fold in the flour and coconut, then scrape the mixture into the tin.

- Bake the cake for 45–55 minutes or until a skewer inserted in the centre comes out clean.

- Transfer the cake to a wire rack and leave to cool completely.

- Melt the chocolate in a microwave or bain-marie, then pour it over the cake. Smooth the sides with a palette knife and leave to set before serving.

TOP TIP
Reserve some of the coconut to sprinkle over the finished cake.

White Chocolate Loaf Cake

SERVES 8

PREPARATION TIME 15 MINUTES

COOKING TIME 55 MINUTES

INGREDIENTS

225 g / 8 oz / 1 ½ cups self-raising flour

100 g / 3 ½ oz / ½ cup butter, cubed

85 g / 3 oz / ⅓ cup caster (superfine) sugar

150 g / 5 ½ oz white chocolate, chopped

1 large egg

75 ml / 2 ½ fl. oz / ⅓ cup whole milk

METHOD

- Preheat the oven to 180°C (160°C fan) / 355F / gas 4 and line a loaf tin with non-stick baking paper.

- Sieve the flour into a mixing bowl and rub in the butter until it resembles fine breadcrumbs, then stir in the sugar and white chocolate.

- Lightly beat the egg with the milk and stir it into the dry ingredients until just combined.

- Scrape the mixture into the loaf tin and bake for 55 minutes or until a skewer inserted in the centre comes out clean.

- Transfer the cake to a wire rack and leave to cool completely.

TOP TIP

Swap the white chocolate for dark chocolate infused with chilli (chili) for a sweet spicy cake.

Cupcakes and Muffins

Vanilla Cupcakes

MAKES 12

PREPARATION TIME 20 MINUTES

COOKING TIME 20 MINUTES

INGREDIENTS

120 g / 4 oz / ½ cup self-raising flour

120 g / 4 oz / ½ cup caster (superfine) sugar

120 g / 4 oz / ½ cup butter, softened

2 eggs, beaten

1 tsp vanilla extract

2 tbsp milk

METHOD

- Preheat the oven to 200°C (180°C fan) / 400F / gas 6 and line a 12-hole muffin tin with cases.

- Place all the ingredients except the milk in a food processor and blitz until smooth and combined.

- Add the milk a little at a time to make a dropping consistency.

- Divide the mixture evenly between the cases and bake for 20 minutes or until risen and golden.

- Remove the cakes from the tin to a wire rack to cool.

TOP TIP

Decorate with mixed candied peel and buttercream.

Chocolate Cupcakes

MAKES 12

PREPARATION TIME 25 MINUTES

COOKING TIME 20 MINUTES

INGREDIENTS

120 g / 4 oz / ½ cup self-raising flour

120 g / 4 oz / ½ cup caster (superfine) sugar

120 g / 4 oz / ½ cup butter, softened

2 eggs, beaten

1 tbsp cocoa powder

2 tbsp milk

FOR THE TOPPING

90 g / 3 ½ oz white chocolate, chopped

350 g / 12 oz / 1 ½ cups butter, softened

300 g / 10 ½ oz / 1 ¼ cups icing
    (confectioners') sugar

120 ml / 4 fl. oz / ½ cup double (heavy) cream

chocolate buttons, for decorating

METHOD

- Preheat the oven to 200°C (180°C fan) / 400F / gas 6 and line a 12-hole muffin tin with cases.

- Place all the cupcake ingredients except the milk in a food processor and blitz until smooth and combined. Add the milk a little at a time to make a dropping consistency.

- Divide the mixture evenly between the cases and bake for 20 minutes or until risen and golden.

- Meanwhile, place the chocolate in a bowl set over a pan of simmering water and stir until melted. Set aside to cool slightly.

- Whisk the butter and icing sugar until pale, then whisk in the melted chocolate and cream until smooth.

- Remove the cakes from the tin to a wire rack to cool, then decorate with the icing and chocolate buttons.

TOP TIP

Decorate with white chocolate buttons if preferred.

Chocolate and Pistachio Cupcakes

MAKES 12

PREPARATION TIME 20 MINUTES

COOKING TIME 15–20 MINUTES

INGREDIENTS

110 g / 4 oz / ⅔ cup self-raising flour, sifted

28 g / 1 oz cocoa powder

110 g / 4 oz / ½ cup caster (superfine) sugar

110 g / 4 oz / ½ cup butter, softened

2 large eggs

1 tsp almond essence

TO DECORATE

225 g / 8 oz / 2 ¼ cups icing
    (confectioners') sugar

½ tsp almond essence

3 tbsp pistachio nuts, chopped

METHOD

- Preheat the oven to 190°C (170°C fan) / 375F / gas 5 and line a 12-hole cupcake tin with paper cases.

- Combine the flour, cocoa powder, sugar, butter, eggs and vanilla extract in a bowl and whisk together until smooth.

- Divide the mixture between the paper cases, then transfer the tin to the oven and bake for 15–20 minutes.

- Test with a wooden toothpick, if it comes out clean, the cakes are done.

- Transfer the cakes to a wire rack and leave to cool completely before peeling off the papers.

- To make the icing, sieve the icing sugar into a bowl and add the almond essence. Stir in enough hot water, drop by drop, to form a spreadable icing and spoon it over the cakes.

- Sprinkle with chopped pistachios and leave the icing to set.

TOP TIP

Sprinkle with different nuts, such as hazelnuts (cobnuts) or almonds.

Chocolate and Cherry Cupcakes

MAKES 12

PREPARATION TIME 25 MINUTES

COOKING TIME 15–20 MINUTES

INGREDIENTS

100 g / 3 ½ oz / ⅔ cup self-raising flour, sifted

28 g / 1 oz / ¼ cup unsweetened cocoa
    powder, sifted

100 g / 3 ½ oz / ½ cup caster (superfine) sugar

100 g / 3 ½ oz / ½ cup butter, softened

3 large eggs

75 g / 2 ½ oz / ⅓ cup glacé cherries, chopped

TO DECORATE

225 ml / 8 fl. oz / 1 cup double (heavy) cream

2 tbsp icing (confectioners') sugar

½ tsp vanilla extract

12 glacé cherries

chocolate shavings

METHOD

- Preheat the oven to 190°C (170°C fan) / 375F / gas 5 and line a 12-hole cupcake tin with paper cases.

- Combine the flour, cocoa, sugar, butter and eggs in a bowl and whisk together until smooth. Fold in the chopped cherries.

- Divide the mixture between the paper cases, then transfer to the oven and bake for 15–20 minutes.

- Test with a wooden toothpick, if it comes out clean, the cakes are done.

- Transfer the cakes to a wire rack and leave to cool.

- Whip the cream with the icing sugar and vanilla until thick, then spoon it into a piping bag fitted with a large star nozzle.

- Pipe a rosette of cream on top of each cake, then top each one with a cherry and a sprinkle of chocolate shavings.

TOP TIP
Use chopped dried cranberries to decorate for a sweet and fruity alternative.

Blueberry Cupcakes

MAKES 12

PREPARATION TIME 30 MINUTES

COOKING TIME 20 MINUTES

INGREDIENTS

120 g / 4 oz / ½ cup self-raising flour
120 g / 4 oz / ½ cup caster (superfine) sugar
120 g / 4 oz / ½ cup butter, softened
2 eggs, beaten
1 tsp vanilla extract
2 tbsp milk
200 g / 7 oz / ⅔ cup blueberries

FOR THE TOPPING

120 g / 4 oz / ½ cup butter, softened
250 g / 9 oz / 1 cup icing (confectioners')
    sugar
blue food dye

METHOD

- Preheat the oven to 200°C (180°C fan) / 400F / gas 6 and line a 12-hole muffin tin with cases.

- Place all the cupcake ingredients except the milk and blueberries in a food processor. Blitz until smooth and combined.

- Add the milk a little at a time to make a dropping consistency, then stir in the blueberries, reserving a few for decoration.

- Divide the mixture evenly between the cases and bake for 20 minutes or until risen and golden.

- Meanwhile, cream the butter with the icing sugar until pale and creamy, then stir in the food dye.

- Remove the cakes from the tin to a wire rack to cool. Spread the icing over the top and decorate with the remaining blueberries.

TOP TIP
Replace the blueberries with assorted berries for a delicious fruit medley.

Blackberry Mini Muffins

MAKES 24

PREPARATION TIME 25 MINUTES

COOKING TIME 15–20 MINUTES

INGREDIENTS

1 large egg

120 ml / 4 fl. oz / ½ cup sunflower oil

120 ml / 4 fl. oz / ½ cup milk

375 g / 12 ½ oz / 2 ½ cups self-raising
    flour, sifted

1 tsp baking powder

200 g / 7 oz / ¾ cup caster (superfine) sugar

200 g / 7 oz / 1 ⅓ cups blackberries

METHOD

- Preheat the oven to 180°C (160°C fan) / 350F / gas 4 and line a 24-hole mini muffin tin with paper cases.

- Beat the egg in a jug with the oil and milk until well mixed.

- Mix the flour, baking powder and sugar in a bowl.

- Pour in the egg mixture and stir just enough to combine, then fold in the blackberries. Divide the mixture between the paper cases and bake for 15–20 minutes.

- Test with a wooden toothpick, if it comes out clean, the cakes are done.

- Transfer the muffins to a wire rack and leave to cool completely.

TOP TIP

Add the zest of 1 orange to the muffin mixture for a fruity tasting cake.

Summer Berry Cupcakes

MAKES 12

PREPARATION TIME 1 HOUR

COOKING TIME 15—20 MINUTES

INGREDIENTS

110 g / 4 oz / ⅔ cup self-raising flour, sifted

110 g / 4 oz / ½ cup caster (superfine) sugar

110 g / 4 oz / ½ cup butter, softened

2 large eggs

1 tsp vanilla extract

75 g / 2 ½ oz / ½ cup raspberries

75 g / 2 ½ oz / ½ cup blueberries

TO DECORATE

55 g / 2 oz / ¼ cup butter, softened

225 g / 8 oz / 2 ¼ cup icing (confectioners')
    sugar, plus extra to dust

1 tbsp milk

12 raspberries

75 g / 2 ½ oz / ½ cup blueberries

METHOD

- Preheat the oven to 190°C (170°C fan) / 375F / gas 5 and line a 12-hole cupcake tin with paper cases.

- Combine the flour, sugar, butter, eggs and vanilla extract in a bowl and whisk together for 2 minutes or until smooth.

- Fold in the raspberries and blueberries. Divide the mixture between the paper cases, then bake for 15–20 minutes.

- Test with a wooden toothpick, if it comes out clean, the cakes are done. Transfer the cakes to a wire rack and leave to cool completely.

- To make the icing, beat the butter with a wooden spoon until light and fluffy, then beat in the icing sugar.

- Add the milk, then use a whisk to whip the mixture for 2 minutes or until smooth and light.

- Spoon the icing onto the cakes and top with the berries and a sprinkle of icing sugar.

TOP TIP
Sprinkle a handful of white chocolate chips into the mixture before cooking.

Blackcurrant Mini Muffins

MAKES 24

PREPARATION TIME 25 MINUTES

COOKING TIME 15–20 MINUTES

INGREDIENTS

1 large egg

120 ml / 4 fl. oz / ½ cup sunflower oil

60 ml / 2 fl. oz / ¼ cup milk

60 ml / 2 fl. oz / ¼ cup blackcurrant cordial

375 g / 12 ½ oz / 2 ½ cups self-raising
    flour, sifted

1 tsp baking powder

200 g / 7 oz / ¾ cup caster (superfine) sugar

200 g / 7 oz / 1 ⅓ cups blackcurrants

METHOD

- Preheat the oven to 180°C (160°C fan) / 350F / gas 4 and line a 24-hole mini muffin tin with paper cases.

- Beat the egg in a jug with the oil, milk and cordial until well mixed.

- Mix the flour, baking powder and sugar in a bowl.

- Pour in the egg mixture and stir just enough to combine, then fold in the blackcurrants.

- Divide the mixture between the paper cases and bake for 15–20 minutes.

- Test with a wooden toothpick, if it comes out clean, the cakes are done.

- Transfer the muffins to a wire rack and leave to cool completely.

TOP TIP
Replace the blackcurrants with blueberries for a more subtle taste.

Peach Cupcakes

MAKES 12

PREPARATION TIME 1 HOUR

COOKING TIME 15–20 MINUTES

INGREDIENTS

1 can peach slices, drained, syrup reserved

110 g / 4 oz / ⅔ cup self-raising flour, sifted

110 g / 4 oz / ½ cup caster (superfine) sugar

110 g / 4 oz / ½ cup butter, softened

2 large eggs

TO DECORATE

300 ml / 10 ½ fl. oz / 1 ¼ cups double (heavy) cream

METHOD

- Preheat the oven to 190°C (170°C fan) / 375F / gas 5 and line a 12-hole cupcake tin with paper cases.

- Reserve 12 of the peach slices and finely chop the rest. Combine the flour, sugar, butter, eggs and chopped peaches in a bowl and whisk together for 2 minutes or until smooth.

- Divide the mixture between the paper cases, then transfer the tin to the oven and bake for 15–20 minutes. Test with a wooden toothpick, if it comes out clean, the cakes are done.

- Transfer the cakes to a wire rack and leave to cool completely.

- Whip the cream until thick, then fill a piping bag fitted with a large star nozzle and pipe a rosette on top of each cake.

- Lay a slice of peach next to the cream and drizzle a little of the reserved peach syrup on top.

TOP TIP
Decorate with blueberries as well as peaches for a more fruity topping.

Lemon Buttercream Cupcakes

MAKES 12

PREPARATION TIME 1 HOUR

COOKING TIME 15–20 MINUTES

INGREDIENTS

110 g / 4 oz / ⅔ cup self-raising flour, sifted

110 g / 4 oz / ¾ cup caster (superfine) sugar

110 g / 4 oz / ½ cup butter, softened

2 large eggs

1 lemon, zest finely grated

TO DECORATE

55 g / 2 oz / ¼ cup butter, softened

225 g / 8 oz / 2 ¼ cup icing (confectioners') sugar

1 tbsp lemon juice

yellow sugar sprinkles

METHOD

- Preheat the oven to 190°C (170°C fan) / 375F / gas 5 and line a 12-hole cupcake tin with paper cases.

- Combine the flour, sugar, butter, eggs and lemon zest in a bowl and whisk together until smooth.

- Divide the mixture between the paper cases, then bake for 15–20 minutes.

- Test with a wooden toothpick, if it comes out clean, the cakes are done. Transfer the cakes to a wire rack and leave to cool.

- To make the icing, beat the butter with a wooden spoon until light and fluffy, then beat in the icing sugar a quarter at a time.

- Add the lemon juice, then use a whisk to whip the mixture for 2 minutes or until smooth and light.

- Spoon the icing onto the cakes and swirl with the back of the spoon. Decorate with the sugar sprinkles.

TOP TIP

Substitute the same quantity of lemon for lime to add an extra citrus twist.

Lemon Meringue Cupcakes

MAKES 12

PREPARATION TIME 30 MINUTES

COOKING TIME 20 MINUTES

INGREDIENTS

120 g / 4 oz / ½ cup self-raising flour
120 g / 4 oz / ½ cup caster (superfine) sugar
120 g / 4 oz / ½ cup butter, softened
2 eggs, beaten
1 lemon, grated zest
2 tbsp milk

FOR THE TOPPING

2 egg whites
120 g / 4 oz / ½ cup caster (superfine) sugar

METHOD

- Preheat the oven to 200°C (180°C fan) / 400F / gas 6 and line a 12-hole muffin tin with cases.

- Place all the cupcake ingredients except the milk in a food processor and blitz until smooth and combined.

- Add the milk a little at a time to make a dropping consistency.

- Divide the mixture evenly between the cases and bake for 20 minutes or until risen and golden.

- Whisk the egg whites until stiff, then beat in a little sugar until thick and glossy. Spread over the cupcakes, piling it up to make it look decorative.

- Go over the meringues with a blowtorch to lightly brown, then serve.

TOP TIP

Why not try using lime zest in place of the lemons?

Rose Water Cupcakes

MAKES 12

PREPARATION TIME 20 MINUTES

COOKING TIME 15–20 MINUTES

INGREDIENTS

110 g / 4 oz / ⅔ cup self-raising flour, sifted

110 g / 4 oz / ½ cup caster (superfine) sugar

110 g / 4 oz / ½ cup butter, softened

2 large eggs

1 tbsp rose water

55 g / 2 oz / ¼ cup butter, softened

225 g / 8 oz / 2 ¼ cups icing (confectioners') sugar

1 tbsp rose syrup

purple sugar sprinkles

12 pink sweets

METHOD

- Preheat the oven to 190°C (170°C fan) / 375F / gas 5 and line a 12-hole cupcake tin with paper cases.

- Combine the flour, sugar, butter, eggs and rose water in a bowl and whisk together for 2 minutes or until smooth.

- Divide the mixture between the cases, then transfer the tin to the oven and bake for 15–20 minutes.

- Test with a wooden toothpick, if it comes out clean, the cakes are done. Transfer the cakes to a wire rack and leave to cool completely.

- To make the icing, beat the butter with a wooden spoon until light and fluffy, then beat in the icing sugar.

- Add the rose syrup, then use a whisk to whip the mixture for 2 minutes or until smooth and light.

- Spoon the icing onto the cakes and decorate with the sugar sprinkles and top each cake with a pink sweet.

TOP TIP

Swap the rose water and syrup for orange blossom water and orange syrup.

Desserts

Apple and Vanilla Pie

SERVES 6–8

PREPARATION TIME 45 MINUTES

COOKING TIME 35–45 MINUTES

INGREDIENTS

125 g / 4 ½ oz / ½ cup caster (superfine) sugar

2 tbsp plain (all-purpose) flour

1 vanilla pod, seeds only

900 g / 2 lb Bramley apples, peeled
   and chopped

1 egg, beaten

FOR THE PASTRY

300 g / 11 oz / 2 cups plain (all-purpose) flour

150 g / 5 ½ oz / ⅔ cup butter, chilled

METHOD

- For the pastry, sieve the flour into a mixing bowl. Dip the chilled butter in the flour, then grate it into the bowl and mix evenly.

- Add enough cold water to bring it together into a pliable dough then chill for 30 minutes.

- Preheat the oven to 190°C (170°C fan) / 375F / gas 5 and butter a 23 cm (9 in) round pie tin.

- Mix the sugar, flour and vanilla seeds together, then add the apples and mix.

- Roll out half the pastry on a floured surface and use it to line the pie tin.

- Pack the apples into the pastry case and brush around the top of the pastry with beaten egg.

- Roll out the other half of the pastry and lay it over the apples. Press down round the outside to seal.

- Crimp the edges and trim away any excess pastry.

- Make a couple of holes in the top with a knife and brush with beaten egg, then bake for 35–45 minutes. The pastry should be crisp and golden brown on top.

TOP TIP

For a more autumnal taste, use ½ tsp of freshly grated nutmeg instead of the vanilla pod.

Apple and Raspberry Crumble

SERVES 4

PREPARATION TIME 5 MINUTES

COOKING TIME 40 MINUTES

INGREDIENTS

1 Bramley apple, peeled and chopped

200 g / 7 oz / 1 ¾ cup raspberries

4 tbsp caster (superfine) sugar

75 g / 2 ½ oz / ⅓ cup butter

50 g / 1 ¾ oz / ⅓ cup plain (all-purpose) flour

25 g / 1 oz / ¼ cup ground almonds

40 g / 1 ½ oz / ¼ cup light brown sugar

METHOD

- Preheat the oven to 180°C (160°C fan) / 350F / gas 4.

- Mix the fruit with the sugar and tip it into a baking dish.

- Rub the butter into the flour and stir in the ground almonds and brown sugar.

- Take a handful of the topping and squeeze it into a clump, then crumble it over the fruit.

- Repeat with the rest of the crumble mixture then bake for 40 minutes or until the topping is golden brown.

TOP TIP

Replace the apples with pears and substitute blueberries for the raspberries.

Mango, Banana and Lime Crumble

SERVES 4

PREPARATION TIME 5 MINUTES

COOKING TIME 40 MINUTES

INGREDIENTS

1 mango, peeled, stoned and cubed
2 bananas, peeled and cut into chunks
1 lime, juiced and zest finely grated
75 g / 2 ½ oz / ⅓ cup butter
50 g / 1 ¾ oz / ⅓ cup plain (all-purpose) flour
25 g / 1 oz / ¼ cup ground almonds
40 g / 1 ½ oz / ¼ cup light brown sugar

METHOD

- Preheat the oven to 180°C (160°C fan) / 350F / gas 4.

- Mix the fruit with the lime juice and zest and tip it into a baking dish.

- Rub the butter into the flour, then stir in the ground almonds and brown sugar.

- Take a handful of the topping and squeeze it into a clump, then crumble it over the fruit.

- Repeat with the rest of the crumble mixture, then bake for 40 minutes or until the topping is golden brown.

TOP TIP
Replace the ground almonds in the crumble topping with desiccated coconut.

Summer Fruit Meringue Roulade

SERVES 8

PREPARATION TIME 20 MINUTES

COOKING TIME 15 MINUTES

INGREDIENTS

4 large egg whites

a pinch cream of tartar

200 g / 7 oz / ¾ cup caster (superfine) sugar

300 ml / 10 ½ fl. oz / 1 ¼ cups double (heavy) cream

200 g / 7 oz / 1 ⅓ cups mixed berries

icing (confectioners') sugar for dusting

METHOD

- Preheat the oven to 180°C (160°C fan) / 355F / gas 4 and line a Swiss roll tin with non-stick baking paper.

- Whisk the egg whites with the cream of tartar until stiff, then whisk in the sugar a tablespoon at a time.

- Spread the mixture onto the Swiss roll tray in an even layer with a palette knife and bake for 15 minutes. Leave to cool completely once cooked.

- Whip the double cream until it just holds its shape.

- Sprinkle a large sheet of greaseproof paper with icing sugar and turn the meringue out onto it.

- Spread the meringue with cream and sprinkle over the berries, then roll it up, using the greaseproof paper to help you.

- Dust with more icing sugar before serving.

TOP TIP

Use 200g / 7 oz of mixed tropical fruit such as mango and pineapple instead of the berries.

Summer Fruit Compote with Meringue

MAKES 6

PREPARATION TIME 20 MINUTES

COOKING TIME 15 MINUTES

INGREDIENTS

450 g / 1 lb / 2 cups frozen summer
    fruits, defrosted
2 tbsp caster (superfine) sugar
1 vanilla pod, halved lengthways

FOR THE MERINGUE

4 large egg whites
110 g / 4 oz / ½ cup caster (superfine) sugar

METHOD

- Preheat the oven to 200°C (180°C fan) / 400F / gas 6.

- Put the fruit in a saucepan with the sugar and vanilla, then cover with a lid.

- Cook over a medium heat for 5 minutes, stirring occasionally, then discard the vanilla pod and spoon the compote into six oven-proof glasses or bowls.

- Whisk the egg whites until stiff, then gradually add the sugar and whisk until the mixture is thick and shiny.

- Spoon the meringue into a piping bag, fitted with a large star nozzle, and pipe a big swirl of meringue on top of each compote.

- Bake for 10 minutes or until the tops are golden brown.

TOP TIP
Replace the summer fruits with 2 peeled and cubed cooking apples.

Summer Fruit Jelly

SERVES 4

PREPARATION TIME 3 HOURS

INGREDIENTS

450 ml / 1 pint / 2 cups rosé wine

2 tbsp caster (superfine) sugar

3–4 leaves gelatin, soaked in
    cold water

350 g / 12 oz / 1 ½ cups strawberries, hulled
    and halved

225 g / 8 oz / 1 cup raspberries

350 g / 12 oz / 1 ½ cups mixed berries

METHOD

- Heat half the wine in a pan, then whisk in the sugar and soaked, squeezed gelatin. Stir to dissolve, then add the remaining wine and pour into a pouring jug to cool.

- Scatter the fruit into the bottom of a large bowl or tureen mould, then pour over the jelly, pushing any fruit that floats to the surface down. Cover with cling film and refrigerate until set.

- To serve, stand the mould in hot water for a few seconds, run a knife around the inside and invert onto a plate.

TOP TIP
Try blackberries and raspberries in a jelly made with red beaujolais.

Lemon Meringue Pie

SERVES 8

PREPARATION TIME 55 MINUTES

COOKING TIME 25–30 MINUTES

INGREDIENTS

2 tsp cornflour (cornstarch)

4 lemons, zest and juice

4 large eggs, beaten

225 g / 8 oz / 1 cup butter

175 g / 6 oz / ¾ cups caster (superfine) sugar

FOR THE PASTRY

100 g / 3 ½ oz / ½ cups butter, cubed

200 g / 7 oz / 1 ⅓ cups plain (all-purpose)
    flour

FOR THE MERINGUE

4 large egg whites

110 g / 4 oz / ½ cups caster (superfine) sugar

METHOD

- Preheat the oven to 200°C (180°C fan) / 390F / gas 6.

- Rub the butter into the flour and add just enough cold water to bind. Chill for 30 minutes, then roll out on a lightly floured surface.

- Use the pastry to line a 24 cm (9 in) loose-bottomed tart tin and prick it with a fork. Line the pastry with cling film and fill with baking beans or rice, then bake for 10 minutes.

- Remove the cling film and beans and cook for another 8 minutes to crisp.

- Meanwhile, dissolve the cornflour in the lemon juice and put it in a saucepan with the rest of the ingredients. Stir constantly over a medium heat to melt the butter and dissolve the sugar. Bring to a gentle simmer then pour it into the pastry case.

- Whisk the egg whites until stiff, then gradually add the sugar and whisk until the mixture is thick and shiny.

- Spoon the meringue on top of the lemon curd, making peaks with the spoon. Bake for 10 minutes or until golden brown.

TOP TIP
Use the juice and zest of 2 lemons and 2 limes for a sharper taste.

Raspberry Eton Mess

SERVES 4

PREPARATION TIME 5 MINUTES

COOKING TIME 35–40 MINUTES

INGREDIENTS

300 g / 10 ½ oz / 2 ¼ cups raspberries

600 ml / 1 pint / 2 ½ cups double (heavy) cream

4 meringue nests, crushed

METHOD

- Press half the raspberries through a sieve to make a smooth sauce and discard the pips.

- Whip the cream until it forms soft peaks, then fold in the meringue pieces and all but 4 of the whole raspberries.

- Swirl through the raspberry sauce and divide it between four sundae glasses then top each one with a raspberry.

TOP TIP

Replace the raspberries with strawberries, but use a food processor to make the sauce.

Raspberry and Orange Fool

SERVES 4

PREPARATION TIME 10 MINUTES

INGREDIENTS

150 g / 5 ½ oz / 1 ¼ cups raspberries
50 g / 1 ¾ oz / ½ cup icing (confectioners')
    sugar
1 orange, juiced and zest finely pared
600 ml / 1 pint / 2 ½ cups double
    (heavy) cream

METHOD

- Press half of the raspberries through a sieve into a bowl and discard the seeds.
- Add the icing sugar and orange juice and stir to dissolve.
- Add the cream to the bowl and whip it all together until thick.
- Spoon the fool into four bowls and sprinkle over the remaining raspberries and the pared orange zest.

TOP TIP
Replace the orange juice and zest with the zest and juice of 2 limes.

Cherry and Chocolate Fool

SERVES 4

PREPARATION TIME 10 MINUTES

INGREDIENTS

300 ml / 10 ½ fl. oz / 1 ¼ cups double (heavy) cream
50 g / 1 ¾ oz / ½ cup icing (confectioners') sugar
300 g / 10 ½ oz / 1 ¼ cups natural yoghurt
150 g / 5 ½ oz / ¾ cup cherries, stoned
4 tbsp grated dark chocolate

METHOD

- Whip the cream with the icing sugar until thick, then fold through the yoghurt.

- Arrange the cherries in the bottom of four glasses and spoon the fool mixture on top.

- Sprinkle with grated chocolate and serve.

TOP TIP
Replace the cherries with strawberries and top with grated white chocolate.

Chocolate Fondant Puddings

SERVES 4

PREPARATION TIME 30 MINUTES

COOKING TIME 8 MINUTES

INGREDIENTS

90 g / 3 oz / ⅓ cup caster (superfine) sugar

150 g / 5 oz / ⅔ cup butter

150 g / 5 oz / ⅔ cup dark chocolate, chopped

3 egg yolks

3 eggs

1 tsp vanilla extract

1 tbsp plain (all-purpose) flour

METHOD

- Preheat the oven to 180°C (160°C fan) / 350F / gas 4. Grease four individual dariole moulds.

- Place the sugar, butter and chocolate in a bowl set over a pan of simmering water and stir occasionally until melted. Remove from the heat and whisk to combine. Leave to cool for 5 minutes.

- Add the egg yolks, eggs and vanilla extract and beat well to combine, then fold in the flour.

- Pour into the moulds and chill for 20 minutes.

- Place on a baking tray and cook for 8 minutes.

- Turn out onto plates and serve immediately.

TOP TIP
The grated zest of an orange is a classic combo with chocolate.

Creamy Hot Chocolate

SERVES 4

PREPARATION TIME 10 MINUTES

COOKING TIME 2 HOURS 10 MINUTES

INGREDIENTS

750 ml / 1 pint 6 fl. oz / 3 cups whole milk
250 ml / 9 fl. oz / 1 cup double (heavy) cream
110 g / 4 oz / ½ cup caster (superfine) sugar
175 g / 6 oz / 1 cup milk chocolate chips
a pinch of salt

METHOD

- Combine the milk, cream and sugar in a large saucepan.

- Cook over a medium heat, stirring frequently until the sugar has dissolved.

- Place the chocolate chips in a slow cooker and pour the hot milk and cream mixture on top, stirring well until the chocolate melts.

- Cover with a lid and cook on a low setting for 2 hours.

- Stir through a pinch of salt after 2 hours.

- Ladle into serving bowls and serve hot alongside warm doughnuts.

TOP TIP
Cover the hot chocolate with squirty cream and marshmallows.

White Chocolate Fondue

SERVES 4

PREPARATION TIME 5 MINUTES

COOKING TIME 4 MINUTES

INGREDIENTS

100 g / 3 ½ oz / ⅔ cup white chocolate
150 ml / 3 ½ fl. oz / ⅔ cup double
(heavy) cream
2 tbsp orange liqueur
raspberries and brownie squares
for dipping

METHOD

- Chop the chocolate and put it in a fondue bowl.

- Bring the cream and orange liqueur to simmering point, then pour it over the chocolate and stir until smooth.

- Serve with the raspberries and brownie squares for dipping.

TOP TIP
Replace the orange liqueur with coffee liqueur and add 2 shots of espresso to the cream.

Crêpes with Chocolate Dipping Sauce

SERVES 4

PREPARATION TIME 5 MINUTES

COOKING TIME 20 MINUTES

INGREDIENTS

150 g / 5 ½ oz / 1 cup plain (all-purpose) flour

1 large egg

325 ml / 11 ½ fl. oz / 1 ⅓ cup whole milk

30 g / 1 oz butter, melted

FOR THE DIPPING SAUCE

100 ml / 3 ½ fl. oz / ½ cup double
    (heavy) cream

1 tbsp brandy

100 g / 3 ½ oz / ¾ cup dark chocolate
    (minimum 60% cocoa solids), chopped

METHOD

- To make the dipping sauce, heat the cream and brandy to simmering point, then pour it over the chocolate and stir to emulsify. Spoon into four serving glasses.

- Sieve the flour into a bowl and make a well in the centre. Break in the egg and pour in the milk, then use a whisk to gradually incorporate all of the flour from round the outside.

- Melt the butter in a small frying pan then whisk it into the batter.

- Put the buttered frying pan back over a low heat. Add a small ladle of batter and swirl the pan to coat the bottom.

- When it starts to dry and curl up at the edges, turn the pancake over with a spatula and cook the other side until golden brown.

- Repeat with the rest of the mixture, then fold the crêpes into quarters and serve with the dipping sauce.

TOP TIP

Spread the crêpes with chocolate sauce and sliced bananas.

Tiramisu

MAKES 6

PREPARATION TIME 25 MINUTES

INGREDIENTS

600 ml / 1 pint / 2 cups double (heavy) cream
250 g / 9 oz / 1 cup mascarpone
3 tbsp Marsala dolce
5 tbsp caster (superfine) sugar
300 ml / 10 fl. oz / 1 ¼ cups strong coffee
2 tbsp coffee liqueur (optional)
175 g / 6 oz sponge fingers
25 g / 1 oz dark chocolate, grated
3 tsp cocoa powder

METHOD

- Place the cream, mascarpone, Marsala and sugar in a bowl and whisk until combined and thick.

- Pour the coffee and liqueur into a shallow dish and soak the sponge fingers in it, but be careful they don't disintegrate.

- Layer half the biscuits into a serving dish, then spoon over half the mascarpone mixture.

- Grate over half of the chocolate. Repeat until all the ingredients are used up.

- Chill in the refrigerator for 3 hours. Dust with cocoa powder and more chocolate to serve.

TOP TIP

Instead of dipping the biscuits in coffee, use hot chocolate and omit the alcohol.

Sticky Toffee Pudding

SERVES 4

PREPARATION TIME 20 MINUTES

COOKING TIME 40 MINUTES

INGREDIENTS

FOR THE SPONGE

75 g / 2 ½ oz / ⅓ cup dates, stoned and finely chopped

1 tsp bicarbonate of (baking) soda

50 g / 1 ¾ oz / ¼ cup butter

a pinch of salt

150 g / 5 oz / ⅔ cup Demerara sugar

2 eggs

175 g / 6 oz / ¾ cup self-raising flour

1 tsp vanilla extract

butter, softened

FOR THE SAUCE

250 ml / 9 fl. oz / 1 cup double (heavy) cream

80 g / 2 ½ oz / ⅓ cup butter

80 g / 2 ½ oz / ⅓ cup dark brown sugar

METHOD

- Preheat the oven to 180°C (160°C fan) / 350F / gas 4.

- Pour 275 ml / 10 fl. oz / 1 cup boiling water into a bowl and add the dates to soak.

- When the water is lukewarm, add the remaining sponge ingredients, mixing well to combine.

- Pour into a buttered baking dish and bake in the oven for about 40 minutes, or until just firm.

- Heat the sauce ingredients in a pan, whisking regularly.

- When the sponge is cooked, pour over the sauce and flash briefly under a hot grill until bubbling. Serve with ice cream or cream.

TOP TIP
Serve with softly whipped cream folded through with a little sherry.

Rice Pudding with Raisins

METHOD

- Mix all the rice pudding ingredients together in a bowl.

- Place the mixed ingredients into a slow cooker. Cook on high setting for 2–2½ hours.

- Check the rice pudding is tender and continue cooking until it is ready.

- Stir through the white chocolate chips before serving.

- Wait for the chocolate chips to melt slightly before serving.

SERVES 4

PREPARATION TIME 15 MINUTES

COOKING TIME 2 HOURS

INGREDIENTS

150 g / 5 oz / ¾ cup short grain rice
360 ml / 12 fl. oz / 1 ½ cups double (heavy) cream
240 ml / 8 fl. oz / 1 cup water
100 g / 3 ½ oz / ½ cup raisins
½ tsp salt
1 tsp vanilla extract
½ tsp cinnamon

TO SERVE

150 g / 5 oz / ¾ cup white chocolate drops or chopped white chocolate

TOP TIP
Replace the raisins with chopped dried cranberries, which work well with white chocolate.

Stewed Pears with Cinnamon

SERVES 4

PREPARATION TIME 10 MINUTES

COOKING TIME 2–3 HOURS

INGREDIENTS

4 pears

60 g / 2 oz / ⅓ cup light brown sugar

½ tsp ground cinnamon

480 ml / 17 fl. oz / 2 cups white grape juice

1 lemon, juiced and zested

1 cinnamon stick

METHOD

- Peel the pears carefully to maintain shape and be sure to keep stem intact.

- Combine the sugar, ground cinnamon and grape juice together in a bowl.

- Carefully rub the pears with the lemon juice to help prevent browning during cooking time.

- Stand the pears up in the base of your slow cooker, then pour the cinnamon and juice mix around the pears.

- Add the cinnamon sticks, cover and cook on a low setting for 2–3 hours.

- Once cooked remove the pears to a serving dish together with the cinnamon stick.

- Pour the cooking liquor into a pan and reduce by one third.

- Pour the reduced cooking liquor over the pears and serve.

TOP TIP

You can poach the pears in cranberry juice to give the fruit a pinkish hue.

Griddled Pineapple with Vanilla and Honey

SERVES 4

PREPARATION TIME 25 MINUTES

COOKING TIME 5 MINUTES

INGREDIENTS

100 g / 3 ½ oz / ½ cup runny honey
1 vanilla pod, halved lengthways
1 pineapple, peeled, cored and sliced

METHOD

- Put the honey in a small saucepan with the vanilla and infuse over a low heat for 5 minutes.

- Pour the honey over the pineapple slices and leave to marinate for 20 minutes.

- Heat a griddle pan until smoking hot.

- Griddle the pineapple slices for 2 minutes on each side or until nicely marked, then divide between four warm plates and serve.

TOP TIP
Replace the vanilla pod with ½ tsp of dried chilli (chili) flakes

Bakes

Chocolate Brownies

MAKES 9

PREPARATION TIME 25 MINUTES

COOKING TIME 15–20 MINUTES

INGREDIENTS

110 g / 4 oz milk chocolate, chopped

85 g / 3 oz / ¾ cup unsweetened cocoa
    powder, sifted

225 g / 8 oz / 1 cup butter

450 g / 15 oz / 2 ½ cups light brown sugar

4 large eggs

110 g / 4 oz / ⅔ cup self-raising flour

METHOD

- Preheat the oven to 170°C (150°C fan) / 340F / gas 3 and oil and line a 20 cm (8 in) square cake tin.

- Melt the chocolate, cocoa and butter together in a saucepan, then leave to cool a little.

- Whisk the sugar and eggs together until very light and creamy.

- Pour in the chocolate mixture and sieve over the flour, then fold together until evenly mixed.

- Scrape into the tin and bake for 35–40 minutes or until the outside is set, but the centre is still quite soft, as it will continue to cook as it cools.

- Leave the brownie to cool completely before cutting into squares to serve.

TOP TIP

Use a mixture of dark, milk and white chocolate chips for an extra sweet hit.

Chocolate and Walnut Brownies

MAKES 9

PREPARATION TIME 25 MINUTES

COOKING TIME 35–40 MINUTES

INGREDIENTS

110 g / 4 oz milk chocolate, chopped

85 g / 3 oz / ¾ cup unsweetened cocoa
    powder, sifted

225 g / 8 oz / 1 cup butter

450 g / 15 oz / 2 ½ cups light brown sugar

4 large eggs

110 g / 4 oz / ⅔ cup self-raising flour

110 g / 4 oz / ¾ cup walnuts, chopped

METHOD

- Preheat the oven to 170°C (150°C fan) / 340F / gas 3 and oil and line a 20 cm (8 in) square cake tin.

- Melt the chocolate, cocoa and butter together in a saucepan, then leave to cool a little.

- Whisk the sugar and eggs together until very light and creamy.

- Pour in the chocolate mixture and sieve over the flour, then fold together with the walnuts until evenly mixed.

- Scrape into the tin and bake for 35–40 minutes or until the outside is set, but the centre is still quite soft, as it will continue to cook as it cools.

- Leave the brownie to cool completely before cutting into squares.

TOP TIP

Try chopped toasted pine nuts instead of the walnuts.

Chocolate and Pecan Brownies

MAKES 9

PREPARATION TIME 25 MINUTES

COOKING TIME 35–40 MINUTES

INGREDIENTS

110 g / 4 oz dark chocolate, chopped

85 g / 3 oz / ¾ cup unsweetened cocoa powder, sifted

225 g / 8 oz / 1 cup butter

450 g / 15 oz / 2 ½ cups light brown sugar

4 large eggs

110 g / 4 oz / ⅔ cup self-raising flour

110 g / 4 oz / ¾ cup pecan nuts, chopped

METHOD

- Preheat the oven to 170°C (150°C fan) / 340F / gas 3 and oil and line a 20 cm (8 in) square cake tin.

- Melt the chocolate, cocoa and butter together in a saucepan, then leave to cool a little.

- Whisk the sugar and eggs together until very light and creamy.

- Pour in the chocolate mixture and sieve over the flour, then fold everything together with the pecans until evenly mixed.

- Scrape into the tin and bake for 35–40 minutes or until the outside is set, but the centre is still quite soft, as it will continue to cook as it cools.

- Leave to cool for 10 minutes, then cut into squares and serve warm.

TOP TIP

Serve with ice cream, perhaps ginger or caramel.

Chocolate, Orange and Almond Torte

SERVES 6

PREPARATION TIME 15 MINUTES

COOKING TIME 25–30 MINUTES

INGREDIENTS

2 large eggs, separated

150 g / 5 ½ oz / ⅔ cup caster (superfine) sugar

75 g / 2 ½ oz / ⅓ cup butter

2 tbsp unsweetened cocoa powder

100 g / 3 ½ oz dark chocolate (minimum 60% cocoa solids), chopped

150 g / 5 ½ oz / 1 ½ cups ground almonds

TO DECORATE

100 g / 3 ½ oz / ½ cup caster (superfine) sugar

6 almonds

1 orange, zest finely pared

METHOD

- Preheat the oven to 180°C (160°C fan) / 355F / gas 4 and line a round spring-form cake tin.

- Whisk the egg yolks and sugar together for 4 minutes.

- Melt the butter, cocoa and chocolate together, then fold into the egg yolk mixture with the ground almonds.

- Whip the egg whites to stiff peaks in a very clean bowl and fold them into the cake mixture.

- Scrape the mixture into the tin, being careful to retain as many air bubbles as possible and bake for 25–30 minutes or until the centre is just set.

- Transfer to a wire rack to cool. Heat the sugar in a small saucepan until it has all dissolved and turned a light brown.

- Use a fork to dip the almonds and orange zest in the caramel and leave them to set on a non-stick baking mat.

- Cut the torte into wedges and decorate with the caramel almonds and orange zest.

TOP TIP

Change the almonds for ground hazelnuts (cobnuts) for a deeper nutty taste.

Double Chocolate and Currant Cookies

MAKES 36

PREPARATION TIME 10 MINUTES

COOKING TIME 12–15 MINUTES

INGREDIENTS

225 g / 8 oz / 1 ⅓ cup dark brown sugar

100 g / 3 ½ oz / ½ cup caster (superfine) sugar

175 g / 6 oz / ¾ cup butter, melted

2 tsp vanilla extract

1 egg, plus 1 egg yolk

250 g / 9 oz / 1 ⅔ cup self-raising flour

2 tbsp unsweetened cocoa powder

175 g / 6 oz / 1 ¼ cup chocolate chips

175 g / 6 oz / 1 ¼ cup currants

METHOD

- Preheat the oven to 170°C (150°C fan) / 340F / gas 3 and line 2 baking trays with greaseproof paper.

- Cream together the two sugars, butter and vanilla extract until pale and well whipped, then beat in the egg and yolk, followed by the flour, cocoa, chocolate chips and currants.

- Drop tablespoons of the mixture onto the prepared trays, leaving plenty of room to spread.

- Bake the cookies in batches for 12–15 minutes or until the edges are starting to brown, but the centres are still chewy.

- Transfer to a wire rack and leave to cool.

TOP TIP

Substitute the currants for white chocolate chips for extra chocolate.

Almond Rock Cookies

MAKES 12

PREPARATION TIME 30 MINUTES

COOKING TIME 15 MINUTES

INGREDIENTS

100 g / 3 ½ oz / ½ cup butter

200 g / 7 oz / 1 ⅓ cups self-raising flour

100 g / 3 ½ oz / ½ cup caster (superfine) sugar

100 g / 3 ½ oz / ⅔ cup blanched almonds

1 large egg

2 tbsp whole milk

icing (confectioners') sugar to dust

METHOD

- Preheat the oven to 200°C (180°C fan) / 400F / gas 6 and grease a large baking tray.

- Rub the butter into the flour until the mixture resembles fine breadcrumbs, then stir in the sugar and almonds.

- Beat the egg with the milk and stir it into the dry ingredients to make a sticky dough.

- Use a dessert spoon to portion the mixture onto the baking tray, flattening the cookies a bit with the back of the spoon but leaving the surface quite rough.

- Bake the cookies for 15 minutes then transfer them to a wire rack and leave to cool.

- Dust the cookies with icing sugar before serving.

TOP TIP

Add 100 g / 3 ½ oz of glacé cherries at the same time as the almonds.

Iced Almond Shortbread Biscuits

MAKES 20

PREPARATION TIME 20 MINUTES

COOKING TIME 15–20 MINUTES

INGREDIENTS

175 g / 6 oz / 1 ¼ cups plain
    (all-purpose) flour
55 g / 2 oz / ½ cup ground almonds
75 g / 2 ½ oz / ⅓ cup caster (superfine) sugar
150 g / 5 oz / ⅔ cup butter, cubed
4 tbsp icing (confectioners') sugar

METHOD

- Preheat the oven to 180°C (160°C fan) / 355F / gas 4 and line a baking tray with greaseproof paper.

- Mix together the flour, ground almonds and sugar in a bowl, then rub in the butter.

- Knead gently until the mixture forms a smooth dough.

- Divide the dough into 20 balls and shape them into short fingers.

- Bake the biscuits for 15–20 minutes, turning the tray round halfway through. Transfer the biscuits to a wire rack and leave to cool.

- Mix the icing sugar with just enough water to form a thick icing. Spoon it into a piping bag and pipe a zigzag pattern on top of each biscuit.

TOP TIP
Add 75 g / 3 oz chopped cocktail cherries to the biscuit dough before baking.

Millionaire's Shortbread

MAKES 24

PREPARATION TIME 30 MINUTES

COOKING TIME 35–40 MINUTES

INGREDIENTS

225 g / 8 oz / 1 cup plain (all-purpose) flour

100 g / 3 ½ oz / ½ cup caster (superfine) sugar

225 g / 8 oz / 1 cup butter, softened

FOR THE TOPPING

175 g / 6 oz / ¾ cup butter

175 g / 6 oz / ¾ cup caster (superfine) sugar

4–5 tbsp golden syrup

400 g / 14 oz / 1 ½ cups condensed milk

200 g / 7 oz / ¾ cup dark chocolate

METHOD

- Preheat the oven to 160°C (140°C fan) / 310F / gas 2. Lightly grease a Swiss roll tin.

- Mix the flour, sugar and butter together in a food processor until they form a smooth dough.

- Gather into a smooth ball and pat out flat with your hands. Press into the base of the tin and prick the base with a fork all over. Bake for 35–40 minutes until golden. Set aside to cool.

- Place the butter, sugar, syrup and condensed milk in a pan and stir over a low heat until the butter has melted. Bring the mixture gently to a bubble, then stir constantly until the mixture thickens and starts to look like fudge. Pour over the shortbread.

- Melt the chocolate in a bowl set over a pan of simmering water.

- Pour the chocolate over the fudge mixture and leave to set. Once cool, cut into 24 equal squares and serve.

TOP TIP
Use milk chocolate in place of the dark for the topping.

Peanut Butter Whoopee Pies

MAKES 18

PREPARATION TIME 20 MINUTES

COOKING TIME 10–15 MINUTES

INGREDIENTS

110 g / 4 oz / ⅔ cup self-raising flour, sifted

2 tsp baking powder

110 g / 4 oz / ½ cup caster (superfine) sugar

110 g / 4 oz / ½ cup butter, softened

2 large eggs

75 g / 2 ½ oz / ⅔ cup peanuts, chopped

FOR THE FILLING

½ jar smooth peanut butter

METHOD

- Preheat the oven to 190°C (170°C fan) / 375F / gas 5 and line 2 large baking trays with non-stick baking mats.

- Combine the flour, baking powder, sugar, butter, eggs and chopped peanuts in a bowl and whisk together for 2 minutes or until smooth.

- Spoon the mixture into a piping bag fitted with a large plain nozzle and pipe 18 walnut-sized domes onto each tray.

- Transfer the trays to the oven and bake for 10–15 minutes. The mixture should spread a little whilst cooking and the cakes will be ready when springy to the touch.

- Leave the cakes to cool on the tray, then lift them off with a palette knife.

- Sandwich the cakes together in pairs with the peanut butter.

TOP TIP

Add a layer of chocolate spread on top of the peanut butter for extra indulgence.

Sultana Scones

MAKES 10–12

PREPARATION TIME 20 MINUTES

COOKING TIME 15 MINUTES

INGREDIENTS

225 g / 8 oz / 1 cup self-raising flour
a pinch of salt
60 g / 2 oz / ¼ cup butter, chilled and cubed
1 tbsp sultanas
1 tbsp caster (superfine) sugar
150 ml / 5 fl. oz / ⅔ cup milk

METHOD

- Preheat the oven to 220°C (200° fan) / 425F / gas 2 and lightly grease a baking tray.

- Mix the flour and salt in a bowl, then rub in the cubed butter until the mixture resembles breadcrumbs.

- Stir in the sultanas and sugar, then the milk for a soft dough.

- Turn on to a floured surface and knead briefly, but do not overwork. Pat out to about 2 cm (¾ in) thick, then use a cutter to cut out rounds.

- Place on a baking tray. Keep gathering up the leftover dough to use up and stamp out more rounds.

- Brush with a little extra milk and bake for about 15 minutes or until golden and well risen.

- Cool on a wire rack before splitting in half and serving.

TOP TIP
Add a handful of chopped dried apricots to the mixture.

Grape Clafoutis

SERVES 6

PREPARATION TIME 10 MINUTES

COOKING TIME 35–45 MINUTES

INGREDIENTS

75 g / 2 ½ oz / ⅓ cup butter

75 g / 2 ½ oz / ⅓ cup caster (superfine) sugar

300 ml / 10 ½ fl. oz / 1 ¼ cups whole milk

2 large eggs

50 g / 1 ¾ oz / ⅓ cup plain (all-purpose) flour

a pinch of salt

2 tbsp ground almonds

1 lemon, zest finely grated

300 g / 10 ½ oz / 2 cups mixed seedless grapes

METHOD

- Preheat the oven to 190°C (170°C fan) / 375F / gas 5.

- Melt the butter in a saucepan and cook over a low heat until it starts to smell nutty.

- Brush a little of the butter around the inside of a 20 cm (8 in) round pie dish, then add a spoonful of sugar and shake to coat.

- Whisk together the milk and eggs with the rest of the butter.

- Sift the flour into a mixing bowl with a pinch of salt and stir in the ground almonds, lemon zest and the rest of the sugar.

- Make a well in the middle of the dry ingredients and gradually whisk in the liquid, incorporating all the flour from round the outside until you have a lump-free batter.

- Arrange the grapes in the prepared pie dish, pour over the batter and transfer to the oven immediately.

- Bake the clafoutis for 35–45 minutes or until a skewer inserted in the centre comes out clean. Serve warm or at room temperature.

TOP TIP
Substitute the grapes for whole pitted cherries for a classic version of the clafoutis.

Fresh Fruit Sponge Pudding

SERVES 6

PREPARATION TIME 15 MINUTES

COOKING TIME 30–35 MINUTES

INGREDIENTS

110 g / 4 oz / ⅔ cup self-raising flour, sifted

110 g / 4 oz / ½ cup caster (superfine) sugar

110 g / 4 oz / ½ cup butter, softened

2 large eggs

1 tsp vanilla extract

2 plums, cut into eighths

55 g / 1 oz / ⅓ cup raspberries

55 g / 1 oz / ⅓ cup seedless black grapes

METHOD

• Preheat the oven to 190°C (170°C fan) / 375F / gas 5 and butter a baking dish.

• Combine the flour, sugar, butter, eggs and vanilla extract in a bowl and whisk together for 2 minutes or until smooth.

• Arrange half of the fruit in the baking dish and spoon in the cake mixture.

• Top with the rest of the fruit, then bake for 30–35 minutes.

• Test with a wooden toothpick, if it comes out clean, the cake is done.

• Serve warm with custard or cream.

TOP TIP

For a luxurious pudding add 3 tbsp of brandy to the mixture before baking.

Cheesecake with Summer Berries

SERVES 6

PREPARATION TIME 20 MINUTES

COOKING TIME 40 MINUTES

INGREDIENTS

100 g / 3 ½ oz / ½ cup digestive biscuits,
    crushed to crumbs

50 g / 1 ¾ oz / ¼ cup butter, melted

600 g / 1lb / 2 cups cream cheese

2 tbsp plain (all-purpose) flour

125 g / 4 oz / ½ cup caster (superfine) sugar

1 ½ tsp vanilla extract

2 eggs + 1 egg yolk

150ml / 5 oz / ⅔ cup sour cream

500 g / 1 lb / 2 cups mixed summer berries

METHOD

- Preheat the oven to 180°C (160°C fan) / 350F / gas 5.

- Stir the biscuits into the melted butter. Press into the bottom of a large springform cake tin.

- Place on a baking tray and bake for 5 minutes.

- Whisk together the cheese, flour and sugar, then beat in the vanilla, eggs and sour cream until pale and smooth. Spoon on top of the biscuit base.

- Return to the oven and bake for about 40 minutes.

- Once the centre is set, remove from the oven and leave to cool. Decorate with berries and serve.

TOP TIP

Ripe quartered figs and muscat grapes would work well in the autumn.

Lemon and Ginger Soufflé

SERVES 4

PREPARATION TIME 30 MINUTES

COOKING TIME 15 MINUTES

INGREDIENTS

1 tbsp butter, melted

6 tbsp caster (superfine) sugar, plus extra for dusting

100 ml / 3 ½ fl. oz / ½ cup double (heavy) cream

1 tbsp plain (all-purpose) flour

3 tsp cornflour (cornstarch)

100 ml / 3 ½ fl. oz / ½ cup milk

2 lemons, juiced and zested

1 tsp ground cinnamon

2 egg yolks, plus 4 egg whites

4 tsp stem ginger, finely chopped

icing (confectioners') sugar, to dust

METHOD

- Preheat oven to 180°C (160°C fan) / 350F / gas 5.

- Brush the insides of 4 ramekins with the melted butter, then add a little sugar to each and turn them to coat the sides and bottom. Refrigerate.

- Place the cream, flour and cornflour in a bowl and whisk until smooth. Heat the milk in a pan, then whisk into the cream mixture. Pour back into the pan and place over a gentle heat. Whisk until thickened, then whisk in the lemon zest and juice and cinnamon.

- Whisk in the egg yolks and sugar. When it starts to look like custard, set aside to cool.

- Whisk the egg whites to soft peaks. Once the lemon mixture is cool, fold in the remaining egg whites.

- Place 1 tsp of stem ginger in the bottom of each ramekin. Spoon the soufflé mix into the ramekins.

- Place on a preheated baking tray for 14–15 minutes until risen. Dust with icing sugar and serve immediately.

TOP TIP

Add 1 tsp finely chopped thyme leaves to the mix.

Baked Spiced Bananas

SERVES 2

PREPARATION TIME 5 MINUTES

COOKING TIME 15 MINUTES

INGREDIENTS

3 bananas, peeled

150 ml / 5 ½ fl. oz / ⅔ cup coconut milk

½ tsp ground cinnamon

½ tsp ground ginger

2 tbsp muscovado sugar

2 tbsp flaked (slivered) almonds

METHOD

- Preheat the oven to 180°C (160°C fan) / 350F / gas 4.

- Arrange the bananas in a small baking dish and pour over the coconut milk.

- Mix the spices with the brown sugar and sprinkle over the top, then scatter over the flaked almonds.

- Bake in the oven for 15 minutes or until the bananas are soft and the liquid has thickened.

TOP TIP

Replace the bananas with very ripe mango halves that have been peeled and stoned.

Tarts

Apple Crumble Tart

SERVES 8

PREPARATION TIME 50 MINUTES

COOKING TIME 35–40 MINUTES

INGREDIENTS

450 g / 1 lb Bramley apples, peeled
and chopped

50 g / 1 ¾ oz / ¼ cup caster (superfine) sugar

1 tbsp cornflour (cornstarch)

FOR THE PASTRY

200 g / 7 oz / 1 ⅓ cups plain (all-purpose)
flour

100 g / 3 ½ oz / ½ cup butter, cubed
and chilled

FOR THE CRUMBLE

150 g / 5 oz / ⅔ cup butter

100 g / 3 ½ oz / ⅔ cup plain (all-purpose)
flour

50 g / 1 ¾ oz / ½ cup ground almonds

75 g / 2 ½ oz / ½ cup light brown sugar

METHOD

- Preheat the oven to 200°C (180°C fan)
  / 390F / gas 6.

- To make the pastry, sieve the flour into
  a mixing bowl, then rub in the butter until
  the mixture resembles fine breadcrumbs.

- Stir in just enough cold water to bring the
  pastry together into a pliable dough, then
  chill for 30 minutes.

- To make the filling, mix the chopped
  apple with the sugar and cornflour.

- Roll out the pastry on a floured surface
  and use it to line a 23 cm (9 in) round pie
  dish. Spoon in the apples and level the top.

- To make the crumble topping, rub the
  butter into the flour, then stir in the
  almonds and sugar.

- Take handfuls of the topping and squeeze
  it into a clump, then crumble it over
  the apple.

- Bake the tart for 35–40 minutes until the
  crumble is golden brown. Leave to cool for
  20 minutes before cutting.

TOP TIP
Use ½ apple and ½ pear
for your fruit filling and
add 4 tbsp of raisins
to the mixture.

Pear and Almond Tart

SERVES 8

PREPARATION TIME 45 MINUTES

COOKING TIME 25 MINUTES

INGREDIENTS

150 g / 5 ½ oz / 1 ½ cups ground almonds

150 g / 5 ½ oz / ⅔ cup butter, softened

150 g / 5 ½ oz / ⅔ cup caster (superfine) sugar

2 large eggs

2 tbsp plain (all-purpose) flour

1 pastry case

4 pears, cored and quartered

4 tbsp apricot jam (jelly)

2 tbsp flaked (slivered) almonds

METHOD

- Preheat the oven to 200°C (180°C fan) / 390F / gas 6.

- Whisk together the almonds, butter, sugar, eggs and flour until smoothly whipped and spoon the mixture into the pastry case.

- Press the pear quarters into the frangipane and bake the tart for 25 minutes or until the frangipane is cooked through.

- Heat the apricot jam until runny and brush it over the pears, then sprinkle with flaked almonds.

TOP TIP

Top with dried apricots and then brush over with the jam.

Apricot Lattice Tart

SERVES 8

PREPARATION TIME 50 MINUTES

COOKING TIME 35–45 MINUTES

INGREDIENTS

450 g / 1 lb apricots, stoned and halved

50 g / 1 ¾ oz / ¼ cup caster (superfine) sugar

FOR THE PASTRY

200 g / 7 oz / ⅓ cup plain (all-purpose) flour

100 g / 3 ½ oz / ½ cup butter, cubed
    and chilled

1 egg, beaten

2 tbsp caster (superfine) sugar

METHOD

- Preheat the oven to 200°C (180°C fan) / 390F / gas 6.

- To make the pastry, sieve the flour into a mixing bowl, then rub in the butter until the mixture resembles fine breadcrumbs.

- Stir in just enough cold water to bring the pastry together into a pliable dough, then chill for 30 minutes.

- Mix the chopped apricots with the sugar.

- Roll out the pastry on a floured surface and use it to line a 23 cm (9 in) round pie dish. Trim the edges and reserve.

- Spoon in the apricots and level the top.

- Roll out the pastry trimmings, then cut them into strips and lay them across the tart in a lattice pattern. Use a beaten egg at the ends to stick them to the pastry case.

- Brush the pastry with beaten egg and sprinkle with sugar.

- Bake the tart for 35–40 minutes or until the pastry underneath has cooked through.

TOP TIP

Use figs in this tart instead of the apricots.

Redcurrant Tartlets

MAKES 6

PREPARATION TIME 20 MINUTES

COOKING TIME 20–25 MINUTES

INGREDIENTS

110 g / 4 oz / ½ cup butter, cubed and chilled

225 g / 8 oz / 1 ½ cups plain
    (all-purpose) flour

300 g / 10 ½ oz / ¾ cup redcurrant
    jelly

300 g / 10 ½ oz / 2 cups redcurrants

METHOD

- Preheat the oven to 200°C (180°C fan) / 400F / gas 6.

- Rub the butter into the flour until the mixture resembles fine breadcrumbs.

- Stir in just enough cold water to bring the pastry together into a pliable dough.

- Roll out the pastry on a floured surface and cut out 6 circles, then use them to line 6 tartlet tins.

- Divide the redcurrant jelly between the pastry cases. Bake for 20–25 minutes or until the pastry is crisp.

- Arrange the redcurrants on top while the tarts are still warm, then leave to cool before serving.

TOP TIP
Try blackcurrants as a replacement for the redcurrants.

Banana and Coconut Tart

SERVES 8

PREPARATION TIME 20 MINUTES

COOKING TIME 10 MINUTES

INGREDIENTS

3 bananas, sliced

2 tbsp caster (superfine) sugar

3 tbsp desiccated coconut

1 pastry case

FOR THE CUSTARD

4 large egg yolks

75 g / 2 ½ oz / ⅓ cup caster (superfine) sugar

1 tsp vanilla extract

2 tsp cornflour (cornstarch)

450 ml / 16 fl. oz / 1 ¾ cups whole milk

3 tbsp desiccated coconut

METHOD

- Preheat the oven to 200°C (180°C fan) / 390F / gas 6.

- To make the custard, whisk together the egg yolks, sugar, vanilla extract and the cornflour.

- Heat the milk with the desiccated coconut almost to a simmer, then gradually whisk it into the egg mixture.

- Scrape the custard back into the saucepan and cook over a medium heat until the mixture thickens, stirring constantly.

- Pour it into the pastry case and arrange the bananas on top. Mix together the sugar and desiccated coconut and sprinkle it over the top.

- Place the tart in the oven for 10 minutes to lightly brown the top. Leave to cool before slicing.

TOP TIP

Serve with ice cream, such as vanilla or ginger.

Fig and Honey Tarte Tatin

SERVES 8

PREPARATION TIME 10 MINUTES

COOKING TIME 20–25 MINUTES

INGREDIENTS

2 tbsp butter, softened and cubed

4 tbsp runny honey

8 figs, quartered

250 g / 9 oz all-butter puff pastry

METHOD

- Preheat the oven to 220°C (200°C fan) / 430F / gas 7.

- Dot the butter over the base of a large ovenproof frying pan and drizzle with honey.

- Arrange the fig quarters on top in a single layer.

- Roll out the pastry on a floured surface and cut out a circle the same size as the frying pan.

- Lay the pastry over the figs and tuck in the edges, then transfer the pan to the oven and bake for 25 minutes or until the pastry is golden brown and cooked through.

- Using oven gloves, put a large plate on top of the frying pan and turn them both over in one smooth movement to unmould the tart.

TOP TIP

Maple syrup is a great alternative to honey and adds a deeper sweet taste.

Blueberry Tartlets

MAKES 6

PREPARATION TIME 45 MINUTES

COOKING TIME 15–20 MINUTES

INGREDIENTS

200 g / 7 oz blueberries

FOR THE PASTRY

200 g / 7 oz plain (all-purpose) flour

100 g / 3 ½ oz butter, cubed

1 egg, beaten

FOR THE CUSTARD

2 large egg yolks

55 g / 2 oz caster (superfine) sugar

1 tsp vanilla extract

2 tsp cornflour (cornstarch)

225 ml / 8 fl. oz / 1 cup whole milk

METHOD

- To make the pastry, rub the butter into the flour and add just enough cold water to bind. Chill for 30 minutes.

- Preheat the oven to 200°C (180°C fan) / 390F / gas 6.

- Roll out the pastry on a floured surface and use it to line 6 tartlet cases, rerolling the trimmings as necessary.

- Prick the pastry with a fork, line with cling film and fill with baking beans or rice. Bake for 10 minutes then remove the cling film and baking beans.

- Brush the inside of the pastry cases with beaten egg and cook for another 8 minutes to crisp.

- Whisk the custard ingredients together in a jug and fill the pastry cases to three-quarters full.

- Bake the tarts for 15–20 minutes or until the custard has set.

- Leave the tartlets to cool completely before topping with the blueberries.

TOP TIP

Use a mix of fresh summer berries such as strawberries and raspberries.

Lemon Curd Tart

SERVES 8

PREPARATION TIME 55 MINUTES

COOKING TIME 15–20 MINUTES

INGREDIENTS

2 tsp cornflour (cornstarch)

4 lemons, zest and juice

4 large eggs, beaten

225 g / 8 oz / 1 cup butter

175 g / 6 oz / ¾ cup caster (superfine) sugar

FOR THE PASTRY

100 g / 3 ½ oz / ½ cup butter, cubed

200 g / 7 oz / 1 ⅓ cups plain
    (all-purpose) flour

55 g / 2 oz / ¼ cup caster (superfine) sugar

1 egg, beaten

TO DECORATE

1 lemon, zest finely pared

2 slices lemon

METHOD

- Preheat the oven to 200°C (180°C fan) / 390F / gas 6.

- To make the pastry, rub the butter into the flour and sugar, then add the egg with just enough cold water to bind.

- Wrap the dough in cling film and chill for 30 minutes, then roll out on a lightly floured surface. Use the pastry to line a 23 cm (9 in) loose-bottomed tart tin and trim the edges.

- Prick the pastry with a fork, line with cling film and fill with baking beans or rice.

- Bake for 10 minutes then remove the cling film and baking beans and cook for another 8 minutes to crisp.

- Meanwhile, dissolve the cornflour in the lemon juice and put it in a saucepan with the rest of the ingredients.

- Stir constantly over a medium heat to melt the butter and dissolve the sugar. After 6 or 7 minutes the mixture should thicken. Continue to heat until it starts to bubble, then spoon it into the pastry case and level with a palette knife.

- Leave to cool completely before decorating with the lemon zest and slices.

TOP TIP

Use the zest and juice of 6 limes to make this delicious tart fresh and zingy.

Plum Tartlets

MAKES 6

PREPARATION TIME 15 MINUTES

COOKING TIME 25–35 MINUTES

INGREDIENTS

110 g / 4 oz / ½ cup butter, cubed and chilled

110 g / 4 oz / ⅔ cup plain (all-purpose) flour

110 g / 4 oz / ⅔ cup stoneground
    wholemeal flour

450 g / 1 lb plums, halved and stoned

450 g / 1 lb / 1 ¼ cup plum jam (jelly)

METHOD

- Preheat the oven to 200°C (180°C fan) / 400F / gas 6.

- Rub the butter into the flours until the mixture resembles fine breadcrumbs.

- Stir in enough cold water to bring the pastry together into a pliable dough.

- Roll out the pastry on a floured surface and cut out six circles, then use them to line six tartlet tins.

- Arrange the halved plums in the pastry case and spoon over the jam.

- Bake for 25–35 minutes or until the pastry is crisp and the jam has melted around the plums.

TOP TIP
Try apricots instead of plums and apricot jam (jelly) instead of plum jam.

Summer Berry and Mascarpone Tartlets

MAKES 6

PREPARATION TIME 45 MINUTES

COOKING TIME 18 MINUTES

INGREDIENTS

450 g / 1 lb / 2 cups mascarpone

100 g / 3 ½ oz / 1 cup icing (confectioners') sugar

1 tsp vanilla extract

12 strawberries, halved

12 raspberries

100 g / 3 ½ oz / ⅔ cup blueberries

6 sprigs redcurrants

FOR THE PASTRY

200 g / 7 oz / 1 ⅓ cups plain (all-purpose) flour

100 g / 3 ½ oz / ½ cup butter, cubed

1 egg, beaten

METHOD

- Preheat the oven to 200°C (180°C fan) / 390F / gas 6.

- To make the pastry, rub the butter into the flour and add just enough cold water to bind.

- Chill for 30 minutes, then roll out on a floured surface. Use the pastry to line 6 tartlet cases.

- Prick the pastry with a fork, line with cling film and fill with baking beans or rice.

- Bake for 10 minutes, then remove the cling film and baking beans.

- Brush the inside of the pastry cases with beaten egg and cook for another 8 minutes to crisp.

- Whisk the mascarpone with the icing sugar and vanilla extract until smooth.

- When the pastry cases have cooled to room temperature, spoon in the filling and level the tops.

- Arrange the fruit on top of the filling and serve.

TOP TIP

Swap the mascarpone for crème fraiche for a different take on this French classic.

Coffee Buttercream Tartlets

MAKES 6

PREPARATION TIME 45 MINUTES

COOKING TIME 25 MINUTES

INGREDIENTS

FOR THE PASTRY

200 g / 7 oz / 1 ⅓ cups plain (all-purpose) flour
100 g / 3 ½ oz / ½ cup butter, cubed
50 g / 1 ¾ oz / ¼ cup dark brown sugar
1 tsp instant espresso powder

FOR THE COFFEE FRANGIPANE

150 g / 5 ½ oz / 1 ½ cups ground almonds
150 g / 5 ½ oz / ⅔ cup butter, softened
150 g / 5 ½ oz / ⅔ cup caster (superfine) sugar
2 large eggs
2 tbsp plain (all-purpose) flour
1 tbsp instant espresso powder

FOR THE BUTTERCREAM

200 g / 7 oz / ¾ cup butter, softened
400 g / 14 oz / 4 cups icing (confectioners') sugar
1 tbsp instant espresso powder
2 tbsp milk
2 tbsp chocolate balls
1 tsp cocoa powder

METHOD

- Preheat the oven to 200°C (180°C fan) / 390F / gas 6.

- To make the pastry, rub the butter into the flour until the mixture resembles fine breadcrumbs.

- Stir in the sugar and espresso powder and add enough cold water to bring the pastry together into a dough.

- Chill the dough for 30 minutes, then roll out on a floured surface. Use the pastry to line 6 tartlet cases.

- Prick the pastry with a fork, line with cling film and fill with baking beans or rice.

- Bake for 10 minutes, then remove the cling film and baking beans.

- Whisk together the frangipane ingredients until smoothly whipped. Spoon the mixture into the pastry cases and bake for 15 minutes, then leave to cool completely.

- To make the buttercream, whisk the butter, then gradually add the icing sugar and espresso powder.

- Whisk until smooth, then add the milk and whisk for 2 more minutes.

- Pipe the buttercream onto the tartlets and top with chocolate balls and dusted cocoa before serving.

Rich Chocolate Tart

SERVES 8

PREPARATION TIME 25 MINUTES

COOKING TIME 15–20 MINUTES

INGREDIENTS

250 ml / 9 fl. oz / 1 cup double (heavy) cream

250 g / 9 oz dark chocolate (minimum 60% cocoa solids), chopped

55 g / 2 oz / ¼ cup butter, softened

FOR THE PASTRY

100 g / 3 ½ oz / ½ cup butter, cubed

200 g / 7 oz / 1 ⅓ cup plain (all-purpose) flour

55 g / 2 oz / ¼ cup caster (superfine) sugar

1 egg, beaten

METHOD

- Preheat the oven to 200°C (180°C fan) / 390F / gas 6.

- To make the pastry, rub the butter into the flour and sugar and add the egg with just enough cold water to bind.

- Wrap the dough in cling film and chill for 30 minutes, then roll out on a floured surface.

- Use the pastry to line a 23 cm (9 in) loose-bottomed tart tin and trim the edges.

- Prick the pastry with a fork, line with cling film and fill with baking beans or rice.

- Bake for 10 minutes, then remove the cling film and baking beans and cook for another 8 minutes to crisp.

- Heat the cream to simmering point, then pour it over the chocolate and stir until smooth.

- Add the butter and blend it in with a stick blender.

- Pour the ganache into the pastry case and level the top with a palette knife.

- Leave the ganache to cool and set for at least 2 hours before cutting and serving.

TOP TIP

After adding the butter to the ganache mixture, drizzle in 2 tbsp of rum for a richer tart.

Chocolate and Walnut Tart

SERVES 8

PREPARATION TIME 25 MINUTES

COOKING TIME 18 MINUTES

INGREDIENTS

250 ml / 9 fl. oz / 1 cup double (heavy) cream

250 g / 9 oz dark chocolate (minimum 60% cocoa solids), chopped

55 g / 2 oz / ¼ cup butter, softened

150 g / 5 ½ oz / 1 ¼ cups walnuts, chopped

FOR THE PASTRY

100 g / 3 ½ oz / ½ cup butter, cubed

200 g / 7 oz / 1 ⅓ cups plain (all-purpose) flour

55 g / 2 oz / ¼ cup light brown sugar

1 egg, beaten

METHOD

- Preheat the oven to 200°C (180°C fan) / 390F / gas 6.

- To make the pastry, rub the butter into the flour and sugar and add the egg with just enough cold water to bind.

- Wrap the dough in cling film and chill for 30 minutes, then roll out on a floured surface.

- Use the pastry to line a 23 cm (9 in) loose-bottomed tart tin and trim the edges.

- Prick the pastry with a fork, line with cling film and fill with baking beans or rice.

- Bake for 10 minutes, then remove the cling film and baking beans and cook for another 8 minutes to crisp.

- Heat the cream to simmering point, then pour it over the chocolate and stir until smooth.

- Add the butter and blend it in with a stick blender.

- Scatter the walnuts over the bottom of the pastry case, then pour in the ganache and level the top with a palette knife.

- Leave the ganache to cool and set for at least 2 hours before cutting and serving.

TOP TIP

You can swap the walnuts for pistachios in this rich and delicious tart.

INDEX